# KARATE-DO

# Karate-do

## The Way of the Empty Hand

EDDIE FERRIE

**The Crowood Press**

First published in 1996 by
The Crowood Press Ltd
Ramsbury, Marlborough
Wiltshire SN8 2HR

© Eddie Ferrie 1996

**British Library Cataloguing in Publication Data**
A catalogue record for this book is available from the British Library

All photographs by Eddie Ferrie, except figure 11, by Mark Wohlwender, and figures 173 and 243 by Tim Green.
Line drawings by Jesus Jaén Escalante and Eddie Ferrie.

ISBN 1 85223 965 4

**Dedicated to my daughters Alexandra and Maria for the continual inspiration they provide and their Great Aunt Nan in Australia, who introduced me to H.G. Wells.**

**Acknowledgements**
This book would not have been produced without the co-operation and assistance of certain people. Firstly I would like to thank my friend Felisissimo Diez Palacios and his student Juan Bautista Bernal Salguero for their excellent demonstrations of Shotokan karate techniques and for the use of the superb dojo facilities at *Kime*. I must also thank my good friend Dennis Oakes for his help in organizing photographic sesions and assisting in solving all sorts of problems. Thanks also to Diego García Aguilar for helping to clarify some tricky technical points and to Alvaro Ordoñez Gonzalez and Andrés Gonzalez Clavijo for being so willing and enthusiastic in their demonstrations of additional techniques in the Gimnasio Fudoshin.

Typesetting and layout by EMF
Jerez de La Fra. Cádiz, Spain
Printed in Great Britain by WBC Book Manufacturers, mid Glamorgan

# Contents

Fig 1   *Sensei Keinosuke Enoeda, 8th dan head instructor of the Karate Union of Great Britain, performing a kata in traditional Japanese dress.*

# 1 Karate History and Philosophy

*'Karate ni sente nashi.'*
*'There is no first attack in karate.'*
Gichin Funakoshi

## WHAT IS KARATE

Karate is an activity practised and enjoyed by millions of people throughout the world and many regard it as the ultimate form of self defence. It is not, however, a homogeneous, easily defined activity. In Japan alone there are over seventy different systems of karate-do and over thirty others describing themselves as karate-jutsu. There is a marked dichotomy in the complex and multilayered world of karate between those who consider themselves to be traditional martial artists and those who regard karate principally as a sport. To complicate the picture further there is a plethora of styles and associations which co-exist under the umbrella term karate.

There are also a number of activities which do not call themselves karate at all, but which clearly descend from common roots. Taekwondo for instance is often described as Korean karate, although its practitioners tend to dislike the description. Shorinji kempo and Chinese martial arts like kung fu (from which karate is actually descended) are other sister activities which are more remarkable for their common core content than their points of difference.

Because of the dynamic, spectacular and impressive nature of many karate techniques, they frequently appear in film and video intended for entertainment and, although this in itself is not necessarily a bad thing, it does tend to give many people a mistaken idea of what real karate is.

For different people karate is a martial art, a sport, an exercise system, a hobby, or even a way of life based on the discipline of physical and spiritual training. The direct precursor to Japanese karate was Okinawan *Te*, but the roots of karate can be traced back over a thousand years to the Shaolin temple in China and the Indian monk Bodhidharma who taught the exercises, breathing techniques and self defence methods that the Chinese monks of that time needed to assist them in their quest for spiritual self-perfection, bodily health and, indeed, physical survival. The Japanese were responsible for the arrival and popularization of karate in the West in the twentieth century, however karate first had to arrive in Japan, for it was not an indigenous art like ju-jitsu or judo. This comes as a surprise to many people for whom the distinguishing characteristic of karate is its essential 'Japaneseness'. Karate is known throughout the world as a Japanese martial art, and Japanese instructors are held in very high esteem, yet curiously enough, the real birthplace of karate was in fact Okinawa, the largest of the Ryukyu islands.

## THE BIRTHPLACE OF KARATE

The Ryukyu islands are a string of small islands to the south of Japan, off the eastern coast of China. The literal meaning of Ryukyu is 'a rope tossed into the water' which aptly describes their appearance from the air. The island of Okinawa has always been the economic and cultural capital of the islands. It measures 108 sq. km (67 miles) in length and its width varies from 5 to 24km (3 to 14 miles), giving a total area of about 1,256 sq. km. (450 sq. miles).

The climate is sub-tropical, and between March and December there are usually numerous typhoons as result of the warm Kuroshio current that flows up from the Philippines. The north of

Okinawa is densely wooded and little inhabited. Most of the population is concentrated in the south, where a recent economic boom has resulted in the development of a number of cosmopolitan cities. Naha city is the largest of these and contains within its boundaries the former towns of Naha, Shuri and Tomari which may be considered to be the cradles of karate.

Their position between China and the Japanese mainland and their relative smallness has meant that the Ryukyu islands have depended historically upon commerce and trade for their survival. At different times in the islands' history, both larger countries have exerted important political and cultural influences upon them. There is only sketchy detail available regarding the history of Okinawa because the island's archives were destroyed during the American invasion of 1945. It seems that the early islanders survived on a mixture of primitive agriculture and fishing. Successive invasions by Japanese and Chinese pirates resulted in the islanders organizing themselves into ever larger defensive units, combining the populations of various villages under warlords, until the island was eventually split into three separate kingdoms, Hokuzan, Chozan and Nanzan, each one ruled by its *anjin* or feudal lord.

Buddhism reached Okinawa by the thirteenth century via Japan, and in 1360 Nanzan entered into formal relations with China, paying tribute to the Emperor, in return for which young Okinawan princes went to China to study, and Chinese artisans and professionals were sent to live in Okinawa. The Chinese brought with them skills in ship-building and navigation, as well as pen, ink and paper production, administration and ceramic and laquer-working techniques, previously unknown on the island. In 1429 the three kingdoms were united under a single king, Sho Hashi, and the city of Shuri was made the island's capital. These factors paved the way for a golden era in the history of Okinawa.

Making good use of the ship-building and navigational skills imported by the Chinese, the Okinawans began to trade with the rest of Asia, travelling to Thailand, Indonesia, Malaya, Borneo and the Phillipines, as well as to China, Korea and Japan. Trade flourished and it became a major port and commercial trading centre for a host of rare goods, from rhinoceros horn to snuff.

The first Sho dynasty collapsed at around the end of 1470, and after a seven year period of political instability and minor skirmishes among rival warlords, the second Sho dynasty was established by the king Sho Shin, who was to reign from 1477 to 1526. Sho Shin founded a Confucianist state and banned feudalism. One of his first edicts was to ban the wearing of swords and to make the private possession of large quantities of weapons illegal. He brought the warlords under control by collecting all their weapons and storing them in his castle, and insisting that they themselves had to come and live near him at Shuri.

The banning of bladed weapons among the aristocratic warrior classes had some interesting consequences, not least of which was the evolution of methods of using everyday implements that were not designed for use in fighting as weapons. The Okinawan *rokushakubo* or six foot staff, the *tonfa*, a pair of rice-grinding handles, the *kama*, a pair of short-handled sickles, and the *nunchaku*, a threshing instrument, were all basically of agricultural use. The other popular Okinawan weapon, the *sai*, is of uncertain origin – it was probably imported from Indonesia – and may be regarded as a kind of dagger in disguise, being pointed but having no blade.

## GICHIN FUNAKOSHI

The word karate is a composite of two *kanji*, the characters used by the Japanese for writing, meaning 'empty' and 'hand' and was initially used to describe a system of unarmed fighting which was brought to Japan from Okinawa by Gichin Funakoshi. Funakoshi was a student of Sokon Matsumura who taught Shorin Ryu, Shorin being the Japanese word for Shaolin. Funakoshi also trained under Anko Itosu, who was also one of

*Fig 2    Funakoshi Gichin, the man who brought karate to Japan from Okinawa and the founder of the Shotokan karate school in Japan.*

Matsumura's students. He was a school teacher and a literate, highly intelligent man, and it was largely because of these qualities that he was invited to go and demonstrate karate in Japan by the Ministry of Education.

The Japanese ministry made the approach to Funakoshi because a quick-witted doctor, who was responsible for checking the physical health of Okinawan conscripts recruited into the imperial army, had noticed extraordinarily good physical development among many of the islanders and had discovered that the common factor was that they trained in *Te*. Traditionally the islanders distinguished between three types of *Te*: *Naha-te*,

*Shuri-te* and *Tomari-te*. These names referred to the systems practised in the towns of Naha, Shuri and Tomari. There is now such a proliferation of different ryu – schools or styles of karate – on Okinawa that these old categories are not very relevant, especially since all three towns are now encompassed by Naha city.

The translation of karate as 'empty hand', and the subsequent understanding of it as an unarmed self defence system, is by no means the whole story. The martial system practised on Okinawa was originally known as *Ti* and was later Japanized to *Te*, meaning hand. By the late eighteenth to early nineteenth century, more and

*Fig 3    A Chinese statue of the later Ming Dynasty of the demon Yen-lo, the Lord of Hell, in a typical martial pose. Did the sculptor intend to represent a flying side-kick?*

more contact with China led to an increasing adoption of Chinese martial arts on the island. A Chinese visitor called Kusanku (or Koso Kun) demonstrated and later taught Chuan-fa, or Chinese boxing and grappling, which the islanders loved and named *Tode*. *To* was the ideogram for *Tang*, meaning the Chinese men of the T'ang dynasty and *de* a corruption of *te* meaning hand, so 'Chinese hand' was what the Okinawans called this system. (There is a modern Korean system named Tang soo do which explicitly acknowledges this etymology.) The term was replaced by karate-jutsu in the twentieth century, but the ideogram used to represent the sound '*kara*' was the original ideogram which could also be read '*To*' and meant 'Chinese', not 'empty' and the literal meaning of karate-jutsu was 'Chinese hand art'. This name was arrived at after much discussion among the leading exponents of the various schools and was considered to be the most suitable because it combined the Chinese (*kara*) Okinawan (*te*) and Japanese (*jutsu*) strands very cleverly.

The *Te* practised on Okinawa even after being renamed karate-jutsu is almost always accompanied by some form of weapons training. However, when Master Funakoshi gave the first karate demonstration in Japan in 1922, and began teaching and lecturing throughout the country at various universities and at the Kodokan (the headquarters of judo, at the invitation of judo's founder Dr. Kano Jigoro), he changed the ideogram for '*kara*', meaning 'Chinese' to one meaning 'empty' so the spoken name of karate was preserved but its meaning was changed from Chinese hand to empty hand. Westerners are often surprised that kanji can be read with different meanings and find the notion complicated, but if we hear the words sea and see, which are homophones, words that sound identical, we only really know their meaning in context or when written down. Other words are homographs such as read (the present tense of the verb to read) and read, (the past tense pronounced 'red') written identically but pronounced differently and, again, we only know the right pronunciation for such words in context. Funakoshi then did not actually change the name to conceal his art's Chinese origins, he changed its meaning.

The majority of Funakoshi's audiences were middle class professionals, lawyers, doctors, artists and accountants, who tended to do little physical training. He presented karate as a system of training for mind and body which could improve even the weakest physique. He allowed individuals to attempt to throw, punch or kick him at will, always defending himself easily and impressing his spectators with his poise and control. Later, in 1935, he also followed Kano's example by dropping the *jutsu* suffix, and added the word *do*, giving his art *budo* status as a vehicle for self perfection, rather than representing it simply as a system of self defence. There were numerous reasons for this, but the main one was to enhance the respectability of the art in the eyes of the extremely nationalistic and patriotic Japanese . To do this it had to be  made into and presented as a truly Japanese art.

Although China has historically been the source of much of the cultural and technological development and innovation in Japan, there was strong anti-Chinese sentiment at the time so it was not politically prudent to attempt to popularize something with a Chinese flavour among the xenophobic Japanese middle and upper classes. Some exponents of karate distinguish between the terms karate and karate do. The addition of the *do* suffix to the word is highly significant and indicates the *budo* nature of the art. The different *budo* forms of martial arts grew out of the need for training systems which, rather than just offering pure, practical self defence techniques, provided a framework of spiritual and personal discipline that could provide a way to self improvement and, indeed, self realisation.

The major change that karate underwent as result of Funakoshi's decision was the eradication of the weapons syllabus intrinsic to the karate-jutsu practised on Okinawa. Many of the Okinawan masters were unhappy with these developments, but, as Okinawa had been under Japanese control for almost 400 years, no formal protest was made and weapons training continued on Okinawa.

The benefits of training in karate as a sport or for self defence purposes are numerous, but for some the pursuit of karate-do offers so much more. There are those who choose to devote themselves to a form of ascetic warrior training called *shugyo*, an extremely arduous discipline intended to take the trainee to a state of self realization called *Makato* or 'pure mind'. This is part of the real *do* or 'way' process and it is the process that real masters, in the traditional sense, of karate and other martial arts have to undergo. The process has its roots in *Zen* Buddhism and requires a commitment of religious intensity in order to bring about an abnegation of self and arrive at an egoless state where action is unplanned, appropriate and spontaneous. Those who complete the training are transformed by it, finding a meaning in life and being better able to understand themselves and the rest of the world,

*Fig 4    A fourteenth century Chinese statue of a demon, used as a temple guardian, to frighten off would-be thieves. Note the stance like zenkutsu-dachi in karate.*

and to control their emotions as well as situations in which they find themselves from day to day. This kind of training can generally only be found in Japan and has nothing to do with the modern sport of semi-contact karate, however.

## STYLES OF KARATE

### Shotokan

The name Shotokan was given to the style by Funakoshi's students, the word '*shoto*' being derived form Funakoshi's pen name as a calligrapher, meaning 'pine leaves', and '*kan*' meaning 'hall'. Shotokan karate did evolve and change considerably from what was practised on Okinawa, but it was largely as a result of the innovations introduced by one of Funakoshi's sons, Yoshitaka, who established the deep, low stances that are the hallmark of modern Shotokan karate. A karate genius, Yoshitaka in fact founded the Shotokai,

11

'*kai*' meaning 'association' which was the basis of the current Nippon Karate Kyokai (Japan Karate Association).

Funakoshi Gichin founded the Shotokan school in 1936, with very high ideals and objectives for his students. Today's Shotokan karate is one of the most widespread and popular styles in the world. Funakoshi's Shotokan style emerged from the Okinawan *Shuri-te* tradition, but underwent many subtle alterations from the original form. Other forms of *Te* which had evolved contemporaneously with *Shuri-te* on Okinawa included *Naha-te* and *Tomari-te*, which, as has already been mentioned, were different mainly because they emerged from different geographical locations on the island.

The defining characteristics of the modern Shotokan style are its concentration on technical excellence and its competition-effective techniques. The sport aspect of karate is highly stressed, and much of the training is competition orientated, although traditional notions of etiquette are respected and the concepts of *giri* (duty or indebtedness) and *ninjo* (humanitarian Buddhism, involving compassion for others) play important roles in the teacher/pupil relationship. The Shotokan style has produced some of the most impressive karate champions of recent years, men like Nakayama, Kase, Enoeda and Kanazawa, and is the most popular style in both Japan and Europe, accounting for about a third of all practising karateka. *Tameshiwari*, or breaking, is regarded as an important test of the effectiveness of technique in Shotokan, and is used to develop and to demonstrate *kime,* or focus. *Kime* is the concentration of kinetic energy at a given point so that nothing is dissipated and all force is directed into and through the target. Rather than simply trying to break a plank of wood by hitting it, the karateka drives his fist or foot through it as if he were trying to hit something ten inches behind the point of impact. This notion of punching through the target and not at it is very important in many other styles too.

The Shotokan *kata* include *Heian Shodan, Heian Nidan, Heian Sandan, Heian Yondan, Heian Godan, Tekki Shodan, Tekki Nidan, Bassai Dai, Jihon, Hangetsu, Kanku Dai, Bassai Sho, Kanku Sho, Niju Shiho,* and *Empi.* As well as *kata*, students practise basics, doing *Gohon kumite* (five-step prearranged sparring, where one student attacks with five lunge punches, one after another, while the other blocks, performing the counter on the fifth technique); *ippon kumite*, where the first attack is immediately countered, and *jiyu ippon kumite*, where the attacker calls out a technique and the target area, but moves around in freestyle fashion, usually in free fighting stance, looking for an opening in his partner's defences or a lapse in his concentration. The defender for his part must look for the opportunity to apply a simultaneous block and counter, given that he already knows which technique is coming and where it will be aimed. Finally, when students have reached a level of technical competence where they can safely control both their techniques and their enthusiasm, they do full free sparring or *jiyu kumite*, where the aim is to fight against your opponent and score with your own techniques without being hit as you do so.

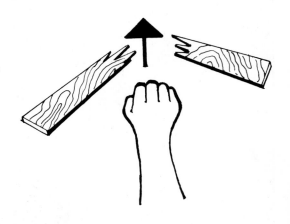

*Fig 5    Kime, or focus, the concentration of power into a small area, is a fundamental principle of karate technique.*

*Fig 6    Frank Brennan, top Shotokan stylist and many times kata champion of the KUGB, performing kata at a National Championships.*

*Fig 7    Sensei Moriho Higaonna, 8th dan Okinawan Goju-Ryu, leading a class in punching exercises.*

## Shotokai

The Shotokai is a much smaller, but still important, branch of the original Shotokan, and was founded by traditionally-minded karateka, including Hionishi, Oshima and Egami, who rejected what they regarded as being the commercialism of the Japan Karate Association with its emphasis on sporting aspects, in favour of a more elitist approach, based upon more traditional *budo* lines.

## Shito-ryu

Other popular styles of Okinawan karate arrived and flourished in Japan shortly after Funakoshi. Kenwa Mabuni founded his own style in 1928, which, like Funakoshi's, was based on the *Shuri-te* taught by Yasusune Itosu, and derived from the teachings of master Munehide Matsumura. It was vastly different, however, to what Funakoshi taught. After originally calling his style the *Hanko* (Half heart) he changed the name to *Shito*. This name derived from alternate readings of the ideograms of his teachers Itosu (*Shi* for *ito*) and Higaonna (*to* for *Higa*). This style and amalgam of *Shorin* and *Shorei ryu* is one of the major forms of karate in Japan and is called Shito-ryu. It contains numerous throws and employs some locking techniques, as well as making good use of scooping and pressing blocks more than some other styles.

## Goju-Ryu

At the same time time as Funakoshi was introducing karate to the Japanese public, on Okinawa a teacher called Chojin Myagi was teaching a Japanese student named Yamaguchi Gogen his particular blend of karate called Goju-Ryu, which Yamaguchi in turn would bring to Japan. Myagi's teacher Higaonna Kanryo had been the man who brought *Goju* to Okinawa after spending six years in China studying Chinese boxing, in particular

the *Hsing-I* method, which places great stress on internal power and development of *ki*. He mastered the basic *kata Sanchin* first, which is felt by many to be the essence of the system, and the open handed *kata Suparimpe*, *Kururunfua*, *Seyonchin*, *Shisounchin*, *Sanseiru* and *Sesan* later. However, Higaonna did not call his style Goju-Ryu, but rather named it Shorei-Ryu (enlightened spirit school). The style apparently received the name Goju-Ryu after a demonstration given at the Nippon Dai Butokukai. One of Myagi's top students, Jinan Shinzato, was asked the name of the style that his teacher was demonstrating by an official and did not know what to reply – on Okinawa most practitioners called what they did *Te*, the obsession with names and styles being a more recent development that accompanied the proliferation of styles. When Myagi was consulted, he replied with his favourite line from the Kenpo Haku, the Chinese boxing manual he was forever studying, "Goju don tosu" which, roughly translated, means "Hard soft, spit swallow, breathe in breathe out." So the style was named Goju-Ryu almost in passing. Myagi added the katas *Tensho*, *Gekisai ichi*, *Gekisai ni* and *Saifua* to those that he had been taught by Higaonna. These twelve *kata* became the basis of the Goju-Ryu and are still practised today.

Goju-Ryu techniques combine strength and hardness with softness and flexibility, mixing internal and external training methods. Breathing techniques develop internal power and slow, dynamic tension movements are important components of the system, as is weight training with a variety of traditional exercise equipment designed to strengthen the body. Yamaguchi sensei, being a Shinto mystic, also attached great importance to meditation. He died in 1989, but the Goju-Ryu style continues to flourish.

## Wado-Ryu

The Wado Ryu, or School of the Way of Peace, was founded by Hidenori Otsuka in 1939. Otsuka was a student of Funakoshi for many years but was already an expert in ju-jitsu when he turned to karate. He had reached the *Menkyo* (license) level of proficiency in Shindo Yoshin Ryu ju-jitsu at the age of twenty-nine, having practised and studied from the age of six with sensei Tatsusaburo Nakayama. Wado is perhaps the purest form of Japanese karate as a consequence of Otsuka sensei's depth of knowledge and experience in the classical *bujutsu*. Wado Ryu karate-do was conceived as a spiritual discipline and its disciples were expected to adhere to the philosophical principle of *ten-chi-jin-ri-do* (heaven-earth-man-principle-way).

The Wado-Ryu symbol is that of the fist and the dove, the bird of peace. The declared goal of the training process is harmony and inner peace through *shugyo*, the austere physical discipline that characterizes the classical *budo* and *bujutsu* systems. Because of its pacifist philosophical principles, the display of aggression is discouraged in training, the emphasis is always on speed of execution, correct body movement (*tai-sabaki*) and coordination. Large, unnecessary movements are discouraged in favour of economy of effort, and the stances are relatively shallow, allowing for greater mobility and agility. Sweeps, takedown throws and locking techniques are also practised regularly, making the system fairly complete in terms of its potential for self defence. Practitioners regularly train in defence against multiple and armed assailants.

The original element in Wado-Ryu stems from the fusion of karate techniques with the ju-jitsu principle of softness or flexibility *ju no ri*. Hard attacks are not met with equal force, but are re-directed and dissipated by smooth, flowing techniques, which use up less energy than the harder, clashing techniques of some styles. As well as being a master of traditional arts, Otsuka was an innovator and was one of the pioneers of the

*Fig 8    Tatsuo Suzuki, 8th dan, chief instructor of the Wado-Ryu in Great Britain.*

relaxed arm thrust with quick pull back from the target to better focus energy and prevent the extended limb being caught.

*Fig 9    Wado-Ryu stylists performing reverse punch. Note the economy of effort and the relatively short stance.*

*Fig 10    Shorinji Kempo emphasizes pair form training. It makes considerable use of multiple locks and throws.*

## Kyokushinkai

The Kyokushinkai style of karate was founded by a Korean-born, nationalized Japanese named Masatatsu Oyama. The name means 'heart mind way' and is a *do* form of karate, involving severe, ascetic training based on a philosophy of courage and discipline. Oyama studied *Tang soo do*, Taekwondo and *Subak* before taking up Goju-Ryu karate with Gogen Yamaguchi. He also earned his second dan in judo at the age of nineteen. His study of Goju-Ryu allowed him to crystallize his own ideas about fighting and karate and, after an extended period of living alone in the mountains, training in a masterless, *shugyo* fashion, he returned to society to found his Kyokushinkai. The style is extremely hard and the the conditioning process severe. Oyama believes karate is for combat, and realism is stressed at all times.

The training aims to produce karateka capable of generating tremendous speed and power. Oyama himself has demonstrated the power of his techniques on numerous occasions, even killing bulls with his bare hands. The principle of dispatching an opponent with a single blow, *hitotsuki, hitogeri* (one punch, one kick) is common to many styles of karate, but normally the blow is not actually delivered in competition so as to avoid potentially dangerous injuries. In the Kyokushinkai system, fighters compete under knockdown rules. A blow is not judged to be effective simply because it is delivered with good technique and hits its target; its effectiveness has to be demonstrated by knocking the opponent down. Because of the danger inherent in many karate techniques, there are certain restrictions which some practitioners in other combat systems regard as glaring omissions. Punches to the face, for example, are not allowed as their inclusion in full contact would guarantee bloodbaths every time, given that the competitors do not usually wear hand protection.

Nevertheless, Kyokushinkai is a genuine attempt to make karate competition as close to real,

*Fig 11   Kyokushinkai knockdown championships are full-contact events and fighters have to do a lot of physical conditioning and take a medical examination prior to competing. David Jones of Rhonda, British Middleweight Champion. (Photograph by Mark Wohlwender).*

unarmed combat as possible. Throws are allowed, as are full power kicks and punches to the legs and body. Full contact kicks to the head are also permitted as they are considerably more difficult to do successfully than head punches are. Kyokushinkai competitions are open events and practitioners from other styles are invited to compete on equal terms, but generally they are at a disadvantage because of the Kyokushin fighters' superior body and leg conditioning. Familiarity with the rules and experience of the war of attrition that knockdown karate can become are obviously important factors too. The removal of head punches is felt by many fighters from other styles to play into the Kyokushinkai fighters' hands, but at the end of the day they fight under the same handicap.

The Kyokushinkai repertoire is bolstered by the use of crippling leg kicks introduced by the founder from having made a study of Muay Thai kickboxing. These invariably take a terrible toll on the unconditioned karateka, however quick he may be initially, because they are very difficult to block. Nerve centres in the thighs are targeted, deadening the muscles, and the victims rapidly lose all spring and mobility in the legs, which turns them into stationary targets that are easy to hit. The ability of Kyokushinkai fighters routinely to absorb barrages of kicks and punches to legs and body is demonstrative of their toughness and of the relative difficulty of stopping a man with a single blow when the head is not permitted as a punching target. *Tameshiwari*, or breaking practice, is given considerable importance in Kyokushinkai, just as in the Korean from of karate, Taekwondo.

These, then, are the main styles practised in Japan, but there are many others which are equally valid and effective as training systems. Many top martial artists feel that style you train in is less important than good character and a sincere attitude to the training.

## Okinawan Karate Styles

There is a plethora of less well-known styles on the island of Okinawa, although the fact that a style is less well-known in no way implies that it is inferior. Many traditional teachers confine their efforts to teaching with in their own dojos, without ever leaving the island, and are often not professional instructors in the sense that we understand in the west. Many have full-time occupations apart from their karate activities, being high school teachers, doctors or even chicken farmers, but they are masters of the martial art in the true sense of the word, having made of it something which enhances and enriches their lives and the lives of many others. These men often have a lifetime of karate experience and are capable of demonstrations of power and technique that would shock many of today's top young sport karate athletes.

There are so many styles of karate on Okinawa that the relationship between them becomes confusing and difficult to unravel. They include: *Shorin-ryu, Uechi-Ryu, Jukendo, Matsubayashi-Ryu, Isshin-Ryu, Kushin-Ryu, Tozan-Ryu, Honshin-Ryu,* and *Motobu-Ryu* among a host of others. Many of the Okinawan masters also hold high grades in other martial arts and combat sports like judo, kendo and aikido and are quite happy to include techniques picked up from these other systems as and when they deem it necessary. This eclectic spirit, a willingness to consider what other style and systems have to offer, is very much the hallmark of the progressive martial artists. There are also traditionalists who want to transmit the arts they have learned in a pure, unaltered form, out of respect for their teachers and because they have an innate belief in the integrity of their art. Although self defence is at the core of karate on Okinawa it is also regarded very much as being an excellent way to keep fit, stay healthy and live to a ripe old age.

*Fig 12   Miyamoto Musashi, the master swordsman and strategist, here depicted using two sticks. From a print by the Japanese artist Kuniyoshi.*

## PSYCHOLOGICAL AND CULTURAL ASPECTS

Since its arrival in Japan at the beginning of the twentieth century, karate has been associated with *Zen* and *Budo*. These are two very complicated and confusing aspects of Japanese culture for the non-Japanese, and are often difficult even for the Japanese to disentangle.

The importance of training the mind in karate has always been stressed, but the average westerner trying to grasp the role of *Zen* in karate encounters a huge number of difficulties. Many karate teachers have a simplistic concept of the relationship which stems from the ideas promoted by militaristic, right wing factions in Japanese society, whose philosophy owes more to Miyamoto Musashi and the way of advantage than to true *Zen*. These are adherents to the cult of the living weapon, mind and body honed to

perfection in preparation for the demands of combat. The living weapon approach is fine as a method of preparation for soldiers going to war, but is not really appropriate as preparation for living in society as peaceful, useful, productive individuals. Other teachers, for reasons of their own, make links between karate and quasi-Buddhist teachings or *Zen* that are really recent innovations. Okinawan *Te* was practised for centuries without *Zen* forming a significant part of the training process. Having said that, some respected modern teachers on Okinawa have introduced *Zen* meditation into their training as a reaction to the sportification and commercialization of karate. Of course, in some dojo, unqualified people talk a lot about *Zen* precisely because it gives their karate an authentic feel that makes it more commercially lucrative than it might otherwise be.

Disentangling the different cultural threads that make up the tapestry of Japanese society is hard work and it is very easy for westerners to confuse and misinterpret what they see and read. The aim here is to try and give a clear picture of the different cultural elements that form the basis of the psychology of Japanese karatedo.

## Zen, Shinto, Confucianism and Bushido

Generally speaking, the most incomprehensible aspects of Japanese culture and thinking pertain to *Shinto*, the state religion which essentially is based on the belief in one's ancestors and the emperor as divine beings. Shinto's adoption as a state religion by the early rulers of Japan can be considered as an attempt to consolidate their power by deifying themselves. It is not such an alien concept in the west; various Roman emperors declared themselves to be gods, and European monarchs for centuries, with the backing and support of the Catholic church, declared themselves to be divinely appointed rulers. In the West today, however, few people if any believe that contemporary monarchs are appointed by god, except perhaps in a very indirect way. This is not the case in Japan.

The samurai, who were the aristocratic, ruling class in Japan for many centuries, went to great ends to consolidate their power and position, adopting Confucianism, Zen Buddhism and Taoism by turns to further their ends. These great philosophical and religious movements were subsumed into the Japanese *Shinto* belief system alongside *Bushido*, The Way of the Warrior, forming a very complicated and often difficult to unravel, multiple symbiosis. Over time, various sets of ideas, or belief systems, can be seen to have been mutually informing and invigorating the other. The *Bushi* (warriors) of the Kamakura period for example were uneducated, primitive warriors, who lived for fighting and butchery. Their samurai masters, in an effort to make them more educated, civilized and controllable, without diminishing their extremely useful martial ardour and combative ferocity, used *Zen* in a number of clever ways. Saburo Nagayoshi, in *Nihon Bushido-shi*, indicates how the *Zen* emphasis on liberation from life and death as absolute values, by pursuing the ascetic training in discipline or *shugyo* in order to achieve *satori* (enlightenment), coincided with the wishes of the warriors to prepare their minds for the moment of their deaths. The whole process lent itself to the development of egoless, selfless individuals who, while enlightened, also easily accepted ideas of service and duty to the masters (*giri*) as higher ideals. *Bushido* often claims to be inspired by *Zen*, but frequently it took from *Zen* that which suited its purposes.

People tend to think of the originators of *Bushido* just as warriors seeking a philosophy that would enable them to come to terms with the fact of possible imminent death, but they were much more than that: they were the men who had seized real power in violent times and were determined to hold it. As well as being warriors, they were master strategists and social engineers. It is often conveniently forgotten that under the *Bushido* code, Japan enjoyed almost three centuries of peace, before she was forced by the United States to open her ports to the rest of the world. Japan's samurai rulers did their job well and because one of the main principles of *Bushido* is that of mystification, of obscuring facts and truth, of misdirecting the opponent for the purpose of acquiring an advantage, it is very difficult to get to the essential truth in these areas. Many top European, American and Japanese martial artists have themselves been taken in by what has become a kind of self-perpetuating myth, and have never really subjected some of the ideas that they propound to serious critical analysis or research. Westerners often do not realize either that there is an inside (*ura*) and an outside (*omote*) to all forms of Japanese culture, although they often have a vague notion of 'face' and its apparently excessive importance in social, business or political transactions. It is perhaps naive to confuse the surface reality with the underlying one, or perhaps it is merely human, since the Japanese themselves sometimes do so too.

## Karate States of Mind

The complex inter-relationship that existed between *Zen* Buddhism, *Shinto* and *Bushido* was the soil in which modern karate was planted and grew. Many of the psychological states which the karateka is taught to try and cultivate come from the *gekken*, *kenjutsu* and kendo schools of the samurai class, and were the result of the cross-fertilization of ideas developed over centuries for a variety of individual, social and political purposes.

The master text on swordsmanship is probably *Fudochi Shinmyo* by Takuan Soho, but among the best texts to study to understand the interplay of the distinct cultural, religious and philosophical currents that underpin *bushido* and *budo* are *Go Rin No sho* (A Book of Five Rings) by Miyamoto Musashi and *Tengu-geijutsu-ron* (Discourse on the Art of the Mountain Demons) by Chozan Shissai. Many of the concepts used in karate training are to be found in these much older sources, being adopted by Funakoshi to increase the depth and effectiveness of karate as a martial art and training system. When he changed the ideogram for *kara* from 'Chinese' to 'empty' he explained the change not just by referring to karate as unarmed fighting and removing the weapons component, but stressed the concepts of emptiness, meaning 'without ego'; 'selfless', thereby giving a philosophical, spiritual essence to what had previously only been a spartan combat art. He states his preferred meaning of kara quite clearly in *Karate do Kyohan The Master Text*:

'As a mirror's polished surface reflects whatever stands before it and a quiet valley carries even small sounds, so must the student of karate-do render his mind empty of selfishness and wickedness in an effort to react appropriately towards anything he might encounter. This is the meaning of 'kara' or 'empty', of karatedo.'

Funakoshi used a number of expressions gleaned from the classical *budo* traditions in a similar context, stressing the essential non-malign, egoless quality of the true karateka. *Tsuki no kokoro* (a mind like the moon) was one of his favourite expressions and served to describe a particular state of alertness and awareness. The symbolism is that the mind should be capable of illuminating what is before it, just as the full moon lights up the landscape on the darkest night, resulting in enhanced perception and awareness. In this way the karateka is able to see clearly what is going on in any given situation and is able to react with unclouded clarity. Similarly *Mizu no kokoro* ( a mind like water) was used to describe the necessity for a calm mind that, like water, would reflect everything that comes before it. The karateka possessing this state of mind would calmly be able to evaluate whatever a potential adversary might be trying to do and react in an untroubled, unemotional way, without panic or anxiety. Both of these concepts relate to the control of emotional interference, to eliminate doubt and hesitation. Often, the two concepts are linked as aspects of the one, aware, unbiased mind.

There is a famous *Zen* poem by a former Japanese emperor which reads:

*'The moon casts its reflection unwittingly*
*Upon waters which have no desire to hold it*
*In the pond of Hirosawa.'*

This poem is often used to compare spontaneous natural reactions with the reflection of the moon in the water. The state of mind it symbolizes is known as *mu-shin* or empty mind.

Two associated concepts often used in describing the karate mind are *Zanshin* (remaining heart) and *Isshin* (one heart). *Zanshin* is a wide unmoving awareness, a quiet mind. It contains within it *Isshin*, the all or nothing commitment to attack. One of the *Zen* riddles revolves around the notion of how to retain *Zanshin* or overall awareness, when committing oneself to *Isshin*, self abandonment; total commitment to the attacking technique. In poetry, *Zanshin* is often referred to as 'water holding the moon.' It may be helpful to think of *Zanshin* as the waiting, reflective mind and *Isshin* as the focused mind in the moment of totally committed attack. The other state of mind sometimes recommended for combat is *Heijoshin*, or 'the natural mind'. All *Zazen* (seated meditation) should lead to the creation of a calmer, clearer, stronger mind that can be directed by the will to achieve your purpose in training in karate. It is not necessary to change your religion in order to practise karate, but to understand it and its real value in depth it is advisable to know the purpose, process and effects of *Zazen* meditation. Karate done simply as a physical and mental discipline, like a sport, can play an important role in the individual's personal development, teaching the importance of control, trust, effort, sincerity and many other worthwhile things. For many westerners that is enough. Some teachers will argue though that meditation will simply enhance the process, making its effects quicker, deeper and more complete. Many leading karate teachers have said that karate-do is a way to peace and meditation practice as a psychological component can clearly play an important part in this very positive process.

# 2  Karate Fundamentals

*'Karate begins and ends with courtesy'*
*Gichin Funakoshi*

## FINDING A CLUB

The ultimate authority in any dojo is the sensei or teacher. (In some styles he may just be called the instructor or coach). He is the one responsible for running sessions and ensuring high standards, so it is important to find a good one. When selecting a club or style to train in it is vital to go along and watch a couple of sessions first and it is worth mentally comparing what you see in different dojos before deciding where you want to train and who with. Initially it is more important to find a good instructor than to worry too much about which particular style might be right for you.

Standards may vary enormously and, while there are a great number of excellent instructors in a host of different styles, unfortunately there are some charlatans around who are just after your money or are on strange ego trips. The worst case I have ever seen was a karate club being held in a local school. The individual giving the classes wore a white jacket with black trousers and a black belt with five red tabs on it. The jacket had the words 'Karate Instructor' embroidered in letters six inches high. There is nothing particularly bad about any of that, but when added to the fact that he strutted around the room swearing at his pupils, a class of twelve-year-old boys, who he was making do press-ups on their knuckles on the parquet floor as he smoked a cigarette and kicked them in the stomach it was immediately obvious that he was not the genuine article and had to be dealt with. Such cases are relatively rare these days, but they do still exist.

## A Typical Training Session

Genuine instructors tend to be polite, wear clean white training gi and insist on high standards of dojo etiquette. Students bow to one another at the beginning and end of each practice and everyone will have short clipped finger and toe-nails. Most of the trainees will be wearing standard white gi, though there may be some beginners who have not yet bought their uniforms, in tracksuits or loose fitting ordinary clothes and perhaps the occasional visitor from another style or school, who may be wearing a different uniform. No one will be wearing rings or jewellery that might cut or scratch their partners. The classes will be well controlled and the teacher's instructions obeyed exactly and immediately. They should not have to shout when teaching because their students will automatically quieten down when they begin to do so. Periodically, clear commands will be given, often in Japanese: the words *Hajime* and *Yame* may be heard among others, and the class will run smoothly and without incidents.

Unless there is an unfortunate accident there will be no blood spilled and there should be no sign of bullying or horseplay during the class. The content of the class should generally involve warming up exercises, callisthenics coupled with stretching exercises, basics involving running through stances, punches, blocks kicks and the like, with the instructor moving around correcting individuals' flaws. *Kumite* practice with attacks and counters, with perhaps some *kata* work and free-sparring and a focus on self defence situations are other probable components of the class. Look at the different grades and try to see if there is a marked difference in their levels. Are the higher grades noticeably faster or more flexible than the beginners? They should be and their movements should be lithe and powerful and all techniques should have a crisp, sharp quality to them. By the end of the session the trainees should all be sweating profusely. The session should end with some warming down exercises or stretching, and possibly a short bout of kneeling meditation. All training sessions begin and end with a formal bow and may contain a question and answer session.

## ETIQUETTE AND EQUIPMENT

'Karate begins and ends with courtesy' is not just a hollow phrase. Courtesy and etiquette are very important elements in karate training. Equipment is included with etiquette because there is a basic relationship between the two things.

### The Gi

The only real equipment needed to practise karate is a training suit, or gi. In fact, originally, on Okinawa, students trained outdoors in loin-cloths, which allowed for uninhibited freedom of movement. The gi was introduced when a karate demonstration was planned to be held in front of the emperor and it was felt that it would be disrespectful to have semi-naked people performing karate techniques before him. Originally, judogi were used, but because these were found to be too cumbersome for doing karate in and tended to inhibit fast punching movements, a lighter cotton karategi was designed.

The gi in most karate schools is plain white and is often starched so that it makes a crisp, snapping sound when techniques are performed. It consists of a loose-fitting cotton jacket, a pair of loose, long trousers and a belt. The jacket has ties inside it so that it will not come undone in the course of training, and the trousers have a drawstring so that they will not fall down. A cloth belt

is worn around the hips. The only real function of the belt is to indicate grade, although it can be used in judo and ju-jitsu to throw or control a struggling opponent. The uniform functions much as a track suit: to keep the trainee warm and allow him to sweat profusely in the course of training. It is fairly strong, so occasional grabbing and pulling, for instance when attempting certain footsweeps, is unlikely to tear it. The most important point about the uniform is that it must be clean. In a physical contact sport personal hygiene is very important and the gi should be washed after every training session. Anyone who has ever tried to wear a gi that has been left overnight in a sports bag without being washed or even aired will know that it is a grave mistake. To wear a suit, soaked with perspiration and left in a bag overnight would be a serious discourtesy to your training partners, your dojo and your sensei and might well result in rough treatment being dished out in a more traditional dojo. If you train more than twice a week it is a good idea to have two gi.

### Other Equipment

Other desirable items of equipment are a gumshield, not the cheap plastic kind, which are virtually useless, but the boxer's type, prepared to individual dental requirements.

A groin protector, or box, again of the boxing type, which protects the whole lower abdomen and testicles is a worthwhile investment. The cheap plastic cup type which slip into the jockstrap should not be worn. These can do more harm than good, as they are prone to slip and trap the genitals, which can lead to serious injury if a strong blow lands there.

Padded sparring mitts and footwear are advisable. These not only protect the hands and feet from impact with hard, bony areas such as elbows, but also, in the event of any lack of control in a blow to the head, they will reduce the risk of injury, and in particular the danger of cuts and bleeding, which has taken on a new seriousness since the emergence of the AIDS virus. Women competitors should wear sports briefs and sports bras and if going in for sparring and competition, a chest protector is advisable. Finally, shinpads can prevent painful bruises on those tender parts of the legs for those who do not go in for conditioning. Long hair should be tied back to prevent vision problems and sports contact lenses should be worn if glasses are normally used. On no account should anyone practise *kumite*, competitive sparring or competition karate while wearing glasses.

## THE DOJO

The dojo (literally 'the place of fighting') is the hall or gymnasium where karate is practised. The best ones are purpose built, others are in old church halls, and others still in modern sports centres. What all should have in common is that behaviour in the dojo is regulated by a strict code of discipline, and the sensei or instructor's word is law. Individual dojo usually have their *Kun* or code in a visible place on the wall. Clubs belonging to certain associations have the association's code and others have more individualized ones. Sensei Enoeda, the chief instructor of the Shotokan Karate Union of Great Britain uses a code which urges his students to: 'Refrain from impetuous and violent behaviour; respect propriety; cultivate the spirit of perseverance; be faithful and sincere; exert yourself in the perfection of character.' There are many other examples, though, and many instructors write their own dojo *Kun*, aiming to set a suitable tone for their dojo.

## Behaviour in the Dojo

Traditional karate is often practised in a hall which has a polished wooden floor. This limits the range and variety of training that is safely possible, even if it is a sprung floor. Karate competition, even the semi-contact variety, should always take place on matted area. The danger of serious injury if a person is footswept and falls, banging their head on a wooden, or worse still, concrete, floor should not be underestimated. Even worse, if an uncontrolled punch or kick lands and knocks the person out, the likelihood is that any damage done will be exacerbated by the head banging on the solid floor. Boxing has long recognized this, and boxing rings always have a sprung floor under the canvas.

When I was nineteen I was once knocked out by an accidental kick to the jaw while sparring in an unsupervised fashion with a Thai boxer friend on an unsprung gymnasium floor, which in retrospect was not a very clever thing to do. The makeshift guidelines were full contact to the body and non-contact attacks to the face as we were wearing training shoes and no gloves. All present felt that the impact of the head hitting the felt-covered concrete floor was probably more damaging than the actual kick. The effects of the concussion lasted a good ten or twelve hours (which were spent in hospital under observation) and were accompanied by nausea, bewilderment and short-term memory loss, familiar symptoms to many a knocked-out boxer, and not an experience to be recommended to anyone. Luckily, there was no skull fracture involved, but in the case of someone with a thinner skull, it might have been a fatal accident. How many people even know how thick their skulls are or whether they would be in special danger in this sort of situation? Of course anyone undertaking full contact training and competition has to face the risk of being knocked out, but it is most unwise to increase the risk by fighting on an unsuitable floor in training. In organized competition there is absolutely no excuse for it, and mats, preferably the high density judo type, should always be used.

Students must bow upon entering and leaving the dojo. During a class, no one enters or leaves without the instructor's permission. This is an important part of the discipline and is mainly for reasons of safety. A late arrival must wait at the door until he is acknowledged by the instructor, who will indicate when it is safe to come in.

Someone just walking in could walk straight into a punch or kick and be injured. Once he joins the class, the late arrival has a responsibility to himself and to his classmates to warm up sensibly before leaping into practice, so as to avoid the risk of injury. Likewise, when leaving the dojo in the course of a class, even if you have a perfectly good reason and permission to go early, let the sensei know that you want to go, and that way he can see that you are in possession of all your faculties, and have not been concussed or otherwise injured and are not about to go wandering out of the dojo to collapse somewhere. Obviously if a blow lands, and the person who has been struck begins behaving strangely, inform the sensei immediately.

When the sensei or instructor is talking or teaching by demonstrating a technique it is extremely bad-mannered and thoughtless to talk, even if you only want to tell the person next to you what a fantastic *mawashi-geri* the teacher has, because you indicate a lack of interest or discipline on your own behalf and you distract someone else from concentrating on what is being shown. There is plenty of time for chat after training in the showers or the bar; conduct yourself with courtesy and respect for others while in the dojo.

Normally karate is practised in bare feet, and it is considered a breach of dojo etiquette for reasons of hygiene to walk in the dojo with shoes on. Flip-flops, slippers or even traditional straw zori should be worn when going from the changing room to the dojo and these should be removed at the dojo door. You step onto the mat in bare feet and you should never walk on a mat in outdoor shoes. Sometimes where the training hall is of the multi-purpose type where other sports are practised, the opposite may be true, and the instructor may insist that sports shoes, ballet or kung-fu slippers be worn, again, for reasons of hygiene and safety. Feet should be washed before training and the toe-nails should be kept clipped short to avoid accidental cuts and lacerations which while apparently trivial can become infected and cause serious problems. Any cuts should be cleaned and disinfected immediately.

## THE KARATE GRADING SYSTEM

Mastering karate is not a short term goal. The average individual can reach black belt first dan level in most modern schools in an average of two and a half to three years, training two or three times a week. This is a praiseworthy achievement in its own right, and an important one for the person involved. However, the black belt is by no means the end of the road. Reaching first dan is comparable to passing a driving test: the first dan has learned the basics. This is just the first rung of the ladder, and a circular ladder at that. A first dan may look like an expert to a beginner, but to third, fourth and fifth dans he just looks slow, clumsy and predictable. Masatatsu Oyama, the founder of Kyokushinkai once said 'The way of the martial arts begins after 1,000 days' study and after 10,000 days we may begin to learn the meaning of karate.' Few people have the patience or farsightedness to think in such a long-term way where a physical activity like karate is concerned. For some it is a sport to be enjoyed while young and fit, for others it is a lifetime's endeavour. Some karateka become teachers in their own right, opening dojo and continuing to practise and pass on what they have learned. Others stop training and turn to other activities.

The karate grading system provides short-term goals for people. It is similar to the grading systems in judo, kendo and aikido. However, in Japan, people usually start out as white belts (complete beginners), progress to brown (intermediate), then go on to first dan black belt (basic competence). The creation of multiple, different-coloured belts for beginners was an idea designed to appeal to people who like both quick results and rapid, if not instant, measures of success. It has proved its worth as an instructional and motivational tool for generations of trainees and instructors alike. Children in particular thrive on the grading system and acquire considerable confidence and self-esteem from earning the different belts.

There are occasionally variations in the colour of some belts, but usually, beginners start wearing a white belt and progress through the grades, represented by increasingly darker-coloured belts until they reach the black belt. The grades before dan (expert) grade are called *kyu* grades and the number varies from style to style. In Wado-Ryu schools, there are six *kyu* grades, sixth *kyu* or red being the lowest, from which students progress through yellow, orange, green, blue and brown belts. This follows the same colour order as in judo, although judo has two brown, two blue, two green and two orange belts. Like the judo system KUGB Shotokan karate has nine *kyu* grades: orange, red, yellow, green, purple, purple and white stripe, brown, and brown and white stripe. Korean karate or Taekwondo has a similar grading system with one important difference – the red belt corresponds to the brown belt in karate.

The dan grades take a lot longer to achieve and in many styles there are minimum time limits between one dan grade and the next, such as two years from first dan to second dan, three years from second dan to third dan, four years from third dan to fourth dan and five years from fourth dan to fifth dan. So, to get to fifth dan takes a minimum of seventeen years' training. In many styles grades above fourth dan are awarded and there is no grading examination as such, but the time factor is taken into account by governing bodies! Above fourth dan, grades are awarded on a different basis. This may be as a reward for years of dedication and continued involvement in the activity when the physical capacity to continue to improve has reached its limit, or for teaching, writing books and generally promoting karate. Fourth dan is the maximum indication of physical and technical prowess in karate, although quite often unless the trainee began very young, karateka are at their physical peak at third dan level. The higher grades are honorific and bestowed for continued services to karate. Sixth and seventh dan are awarded to those who contribute beyond what can be achieved merely by training and by taking part in competition. Eighth, ninth and tenth dan grades are exceptional awards for a lifetime's effort and dedication. In traditional systems their holders are always mature men in their fifties or sixties.

Some modern systems have much younger individuals claiming exceptionally high grades. These grades should be regarded in a different light to those awarded in the traditional systems. In the USA, for instance, it is not unknown for someone who is a second or third dan in a traditional style to decide to found his own style, automatically awarding himself a tenth dan as the founder of the style. It may be the case that through good marketing and organization such styles thrive and become popular and have thousands of members and a different emphasis to more traditional systems. It is not valid though to compare such systems, or their grades, with the traditional ones as there may be huge differences in knowledge and ability. In any of the traditional Japanese or Okinawan karate systems, a 35-year-old tenth dan is an impossibility.

In most traditional systems in the beginning, a student training two to three times a week is allowed to take a grading examination every three months. Gradings are important stepping stones in the training process, allowing the trainee to measure his progress and to discover strengths and weakness that might otherwise not come to his attention. Through the *kyu* grades, trainees are expected to learn and be able to demonstrate *kihon* (basics), including stances, steps, blocks, punches and kicks. They must also learn to put these together in prearranged demonstrations of the applications of the various techniques (*kumite*) and learn the *kata* of their particular system. By about brown belt level free-fighting or sparring is usually introduced into the syllabus, the emphasis being on speed, accuracy and control of techniques. It is vitally important that control is learned so that the karateka does not injure his training partners. This is one of the building blocks of the system of mutual respect that makes karate such a worthwhile discipline to practise. Over the years karateka train and develop together as people, as athletes and as competitors, rather than just as fighters. Because there is none of the damaging contact found in sports like western boxing, injuries are kept to a minimum, and it is possible to keep practising and reaping the benefits in terms of health and a positive mental outlook for a lot longer. This is less true of the systems that favour full contact and knockdown styles of competition. There is a tendency, because of the pressure for karate competition to be realistic (for the competitors actually to hit one another), for the semi-contact styles increasingly to raise the threshold as to what constitutes acceptable contact. Competitors and coaches who want to increase contact now argue more and more for the introduction of more effective and better protective clothing and devices, body armour, headguards and the like, such as are used in ITF (full-contact) Taekwondo.

One of the positive results of the grading system is that karate tends to be highly structured and hierarchical in nature. This lends itself to developing the atmosphere of strict discipline that is so essential when training in combat arts that involve potentially dangerous techniques. Lower grades should respect the experience of higher grades and follow their instructions to the letter in the dojo.

## LEARNING TECHNIQUE: BODY POSITIONING AND MOVEMENT

Stance (*dachi*) and posture (*kamae*) are essential elements of good karate. Good posture allows the karateka to react appropriately at all times. Training in the wide variety of karate stances is part of the key to agility and ensures he has the strength and flexibility necessary to move lithely and quickly when he has to. Kamae is really the combination of stance and guard that the karateka adopts when practising or free-fighting. Left-handed fighters usually prefer to stand with the right side of the body forwards, the right hand held up at shoulder height, like southpaw boxers who lead

with the right hand. The left hand will then be held on, or just above, the hip ready to counter-punch, in semi-contact styles, or it will be held up to protect the jaw and head in full contact styles. The orthodox, or right-handed, fighter will stand in a mirror image to this. The left hand will be the front hand and the left leg will be forwards.

Smoothly powerful, effective techniques require a stable base, and the karateka must be able to retain his balance and mobility in all situations. Unlike martial arts which contain a lot of wrestling or grappling techniques, like ju-jitsu and judo, there is no ground fighting in karate. This is because the philosophy underlying karate is that it gives practitioner a system of defence against multiple assailants. You cannot defend yourself against more than one person if you begin to wrestle on the ground, as you inevitably leave yourself vulnerable to all manner of attack. The Okinawan Goju-Ryu master Eiichi Miyazato (eighth dan) who holds a sixth dan in Kodokan judo as well as his karate grade once commented that 'Karate is a defence against four antagonists, not one.'

## *Dachi* (Stances)

The essence of good karate is the combination of stability and mobility that only comes from long and arduous training. Beginners tend to place too much emphasis on the strength and stability of their stances at the expense of mobility. The key to effective movement is relaxation. Only the muscles necessary for a given movement need to be tensed when making the movement. The muscles not involved in the movement should be relaxed, as tensing them up will only slow down the action. It is important to train in all of the stances until it becomes second nature to adopt the appropriate stance to apply a given technique in any situation. A stable, effective base for all techniques is necessary in order for them to be effective as well as controllable. Speed without stability is like driving a car with no brakes.

Fine control is a crucial component of karate technique; it is vitally important to be able to stop a fully focused technique a hair's breadth from your training partner's nose. The notion of the stance should not be misunderstood. In the beginning when you take up karate you will be incompetent and will have to learn everything step by step, so a lot of time will be spent in stances, thinking about the position of the legs and feet, the amount of bend in the knees, the height of the hips and so on. Time spent in the various stances has a useful training effect, strengthening the legs and joints and improving flexibility. Once the basic stances are learned, the important thing is to be able to flow in and out of them, switching from one to another with natural ease as you spar or fight.

Holding the different stances until your leg muscles quiver and tremble may be both hard work and monotonous, but it is a tried and tested way of developing strength and flexibility in the legs, hips, knees and ankles in many martial arts. Beginners always find it difficult to bend the knees sufficiently and use their legs effectively when punching and, to a lesser extent, when kicking but, as their training progresses, this difficulty gradually diminishes to such an extent that they often forget that it was ever a problem. Stance training is a deliberate method of training, aimed at correcting inefficient biomechanical actions. When actually fighting in semi-contact, however, karateka seem to spend much more time bouncing on the balls of their feet in a loose-looking free-fighting stance in an effort not to become a sitting duck; the traditional stances are only really seen in brief moments of transition when techniques are tried and power has to be focused. In modern times fighters are rarely seen moving around in *zenkutsu-dachi* or *kiba-dachi* because in doing so they would be too static and liable to be scored upon. There is a time to be solid and immovable, a time to be mobile and elusive, a time to block, and a time to strike, and there are stances for each situation. Some of the stances the beginner has to practise may seem irrelevant at

first, but after a few years' training, the karateka realizes their value in such instances as recovering from a kicking attack the opponent has avoided, side-stepping and countering lunges, cross-stepping in order to close distance and a myriad of other situations.

It takes a long time to understand fully the importance and variety of stances and their inter-relatedness. Even the most basic stances, the ones first taught to beginners, have their secrets. A stance such as *zenkutsu-dachi*, the forward stance for instance, varies considerably in terms of what the muscles of the legs are doing when it is used for practising stepping and moving and when it is used for delivering a technique like *oi-zuki*. When stepping, the front knee has to bend, but the muscles of the thighs and calves in both legs should be relaxed, allowing the feet to glide over the floor in a light, speedy movement. When a punch is delivered, the muscles tense, to allow the feet to grip the floor and lock the hips into a position where they drive power into the technique. The point of this example is to illustrate that stance is not an unchanging fixed and static concept.

As well as simply holding the different stances for extended periods of time it can be useful to practise tensing and relaxing the leg muscles for thirty-second bursts while holding a stance. This exercise helps develop co-ordination and feeling for correctly applying and focusing techniques. It is a good idea to think about and practise the attacking and defensive techniques appropriate to the given stances as you learn them.

There are many stances in modern karate systems. In this chapter the stances considered are those taught in the modern Shotokan system. The major ones are *zenkutsu-dachi* (forward stance), *kokutsu-dachi* (back stance), *kiba-dachi* (straddle stance), *shiko-dachi* (square stance), *fudo-dachi* (rooted stance), *neko-ashi-dachi* (cat stance), *sanchin-dachi* (hour-glass stance), *hangetsu-dachi* (half-moon stance). As well as these, there are the more natural body positions (*shizentai*) which include *musubi-dachi* and *heisoku-dachi* (informal attention stances, the former with the feet turned out), *heiko-dachi* (parallel stance), *teiji-dachi* (T stance), *renoji-dachi* (L stance) and *hachiji-dachi* (open leg stance).

Mastery of the different stances is essential to the correct co-ordination of feet, legs and hips, which, in turn, provides the key to fast, agile movement. All the strikes, blocks and kicks of karate proceed from these foundations. Many other styles of karate share the same names for their stances, but there are subtle differences in emphasis and many, especially more traditional Okinawan styles, contain stances which are not as deep. The theory behind the deep stances employed by Shotokan exponents is that such training makes the legs and hips strong and supple.

## BASIC STANCES

### *Shizentai* (**Natural Posture**)

*Shizentai* is the relaxed, upright, natural posture; feet shoulder width apart, hands by sides, open, not clenched in fists. The shoulders, chest and arms should be completely relaxed, but a little tension should be held in the abdominal muscles. The chin should not jut out defiantly, but should be slightly lowered and the eyes should be looking straight ahead but slightly below eye level, as if gazing at something in the distance. The body should be relaxed, with the knees very slightly bent and the weight on the balls of the feet, with just enough room to slip a sheet of paper under the heels. The mind must be alert and it should be an easy matter to react to any change in circumstances and adopt any stance that might be required. *Shizentai* is the natural posture used in judo and aikido too, where stances as understood in karate are not taught. It is called 'natural posture' because it is an easy way to stand and is not tiring.

*Fig 13 Hachiji-dachi.*

### *Hachiji-dachi*
*(Fig 13)*
This would be simply called *shizentai* in other Japanese martial arts except the feet are turned out perhaps a fraction more.

### *Uchi-hachiji-dachi*

This is a variation of the previous stance where the toes are pointed inwards in pigeon toed fashion. It is used when practising the *kata Sanchin*.

### *Heiko-dachi*

This stance is distinguished from the above in that the feet, while still the width of the hips apart, are kept pointed directly forwards, parallel to one another.

*Fig 14   Heisoku-dachi.*

*Fig 15   Teiji-dachi.*

## Heisoku-dachi
*(Fig 14)*

This is a form of *shizentai* where the feet are drawn together so that they are parallel and touching one another, with the toes pointing straight ahead. When competitors face one another and bow at the beginning and end of a competition, this is the correct position for the feet to be in. It is an informal, non-bellicose attention stance.

## Musubi-dachi

This is the same as *heisoku-dachi* except that while the heels are kept touching, the feet are turned out at a 45 degree angle.

## *Teiji-dachi* (T Stance)
*(Fig 15)*

In this stance the feet are about 30cm (12in) apart. The front foot points straight ahead, and the back foot is at an angle of about 85 degrees. The legs are straight. This stance is often used in situations where some kind of self defence action may be required such as when you become involved in a discussion or argument with someone and you are unsure whether the person may resort to violence. The front leg protects the groin, reducing the target area on offer to a straight knee or kick without being overtly challenging or aggressive.

## *Renoji-dachi* (L Stance)

This is similar to the previous stance, but the rear leg moves further across, putting you more square-on to any potential adversary. This presents more of a target, but also allows the possibility of a *maegeri* off the rear leg, should this be required.

All of these forms of *shizentai* should be studied because in real social situations, such as in bars, night clubs, restaurants, or bus queues where you may find yourself in a confrontational situation, these are the natural positions you will have to adopt and manoeuvre within while the situation is still at the talking stage.

## *Zenkutsu-dachi* (Forward Stance)

*(Figs 16–18)*

Starting in *heisoku-dachi*, feet together, legs straight, with the hands on the hips, slide the left leg forwards, bending the left knee and driving strongly forwards with the right leg, thrusting it straight until the left knee is over the left foot. The feet should be about the width of the hips apart and the length of the stance should be between about 80 to 95cm (32 and 38 inches ), depending upon the length of the karateka's legs. The ankles and knees should exert force, flexing so that the feet grip the floor, and point the front foot slightly inwards. Angle the back foot so that it points in the same direction. About 60 per cent of the weight should be on the front leg and 40 per cent on the rear and with the heel of the rear foot kept on the ground. The back should be kept straight and the trunk held upright. Repeat on the other side.

This basic position, front leg bent, back leg straight, is the basis or foundation of much of the training done in the dojo. The forward stance is used as a stable base from which to defend against incoming kicking and punching attacks with blocking techniques like *gedan-barai* and *jodan-age-uke*. It is also the basic stance for making forward-stepping movements with punching techniques like *oi-zuki* or kicks like *mae-geri*. It is very stable to the front and rear.

*Fig 17   Zenkutsu-dachi, front view.*

*Fig 16   Zenkutsu-dachi, side view.*

*Fig 18   Zenkutsu-dachi with a spear hand strike in kata.*

## *Kokutsu-dachi* (Back Stance)

*(Figs 19–20)*

From the starting position of feet together and hands on hips, bend the left leg, sliding the right leg forwards at the same time, keeping the hips low. Aim at distributing the weight about 70 per cent on the rear leg and 30 per cent on the forward leg. The toes of the forward foot should be pointing directly ahead and the rear foot should be turned at a right angle to the front foot.

The heel of the rear leg should align exactly with the heel of the forward leg. The rear ankle should be flexed and the foot should firmly grip the floor. The heel of the forward foot should be on the ground too, but only very lightly, not supporting more than a third of the body weight.

The rear leg is the strong leg in this stance and the rear knee should be turned out as much as possible, keeping the muscles of the leg in continuous tension.

*Fig 19   Balanced strength, flexibility and stability are the hallmarks of a good stance. Frank Brennan in kokutsu-dachi.*

## *Neko-ashi-dachi* (Cat Stance)

### *(Fig 21)*

The cat stance is a variant on the back stance. From the back stance (Fig 20) draw the front foot closer to the rear one until the rear leg is supporting 90 per cent of the body weight. Turn the rear foot out at a 45-degree angle and lift the front knee up so that only the ball of the front foot is touching the floor.

This stance allows for quick forwards and backwards movements, for dodging attacks and then springing back into the attack using the front leg to strike with, just as a cat does, springing from its haunches and swiping with its claws, hence the name.

The two photographs below of different *kata* competitors taken at different championships illustrate the essential differences between back stance and the cat stance which many beginners find confusing. Although the angle of view is not exactly the same the differences that exist between the two stances are clear. The cat stance is shallower, higher and more weight is held on the rear leg.

*Fig 20    Kokutsu-dachi, the back stance.*

*Fig 21    Neko-ashi-dachi, the cat stance.*

## *Fudo-dachi* (Rooted Stance)
*(Fig 22)*

This stance is between the front stance and the straddle stance, and is most useful for powerful blocking and rapid counter-attacking. It gives an impression of solidness and immovability, like a deeply rooted tree. Both feet are pointing forwards at 45 degrees, and both knees are equally bent.

*Fig 22   Fudo-dachi, the rooted stance.*

## *Kiba-dachi* (Straddle Stance)
*(Fig 23)*

Sometimes known as the horse-riding stance, *Kiba-dachi* is a fundamental training stance in many martial arts and is used to develop strong legs and hips. From the starting position, slide the right leg out to the right, bend the knees, keep the back straight. Depending on body structure the distance between the feet will be between 80 and 95cm (32 and 38 inches), a taller person having a wider stance. The body must be kept straight and the feet turned slightly in. The buttocks, knees and ankles must be flexed and the soles of the feet should be kept flat on the floor. The weight should be distributed evenly between both feet.

This stance is used when applying techniques to the side and rear, like *uraken-uchi*, *empi-uchi*, *yoko-geri*, and *ushiro-geri*. If the feet are allowed to follow their natural tendency to turn out, the stance becomes *shiko-dachi*.

*Fig 23   Kiba-dachi, the straddle, astride or horse stance.*

*Fig 24   A fine example of kiba-dachi taken at a KUGB National Kata Championships.*

## *Sanchin-dachi* (Hour-Glass Stance)
*(Fig 25)*

One foot is kept just in front of the other at shoulder-width distance apart, the toes of the rear foot aligning with the heel of the front foot. The rear foot points straight ahead and the front foot is angled inwards at 45 degrees. The ankles and knees must be tensed and the knees must press inwards. Tense the muscles of the inner thighs and buttocks. The back must be kept straight and the weight must be evenly distributed over both feet.

This stance is named after the *kata Sanchin*, where the performer takes small, semi-circular steps in this contracted, tight way, while performing special breathing exercises together with arm and hand movements.

*Fig 25  Sanchin-dachi.*

## *Hangetsu-dachi* (Half-Moon Stance)
*(Fig 26)*

As a stance *hangetsu* is somewhere between *sanchin* and *zenkutsu-dachi* and like the former is also the name of a *kata*. The feet are wider than in *Sanchin*, but the knees and thighs press inwards in the same fashion. The stance resembles *zenkutsu*, except that the front foot is more turned in and the back leg, too, is bent. It is a stance favoured for defensive movements more than for attacking movements.

*Fig 26  Hangetsu-dachi.*

## Free-Fighting Stance

*(Fig 27)*

The free-fighting stance is very much a matter of individual preference and is often determined by the kind of opponent being fought, the rule structure and by the kind of match. It often resembles *zenkutsu-dachi*, but with less knee bend, allowing for greater mobility. Some fighters like to have both hands up in front of them, guarding head and body. Others prefer to keep one hand well forwards as a kind of probe or range finder, a little like the way some boxers use the jab, keeping their other fist on their hip ready to launch a counter attack the minute they feel their opponent coming in, relying on speed and body movement, rather than on solid blocking, to get them out of trouble. In kyokushinkai tournaments, some fighters like to keep both hands high, protecting the head against full-power kicks, and punch down into their opponents' chest and shoulder areas.

Fig 27   *The perfect poise and relaxation of an all-time great in free fighting posture. Vic Charles, world heavyweight karate champion, looking relaxed but concentrated, measures the distance between himself and his opponent.*

Fig 28   *In the heat of combat any defects soon become apparent. Basic mistakes usually stem from weaknesses in stance. Both fighters' rear heels lift off the ground at the moment of impact. No score!*

## MOVING FROM ONE STANCE INTO ANOTHER

*(Figs 29–34)*

When considering the mechanics of stances, certain things become obvious. It is necessary to be able to move into almost any stance in virtually any direction, should the occasion demand it. The wider the base, the lower the hips will be and the lower the centre of gravity, hence greater stability. Stances gain or lose stability when the centre of gravity is raised or lowered. Stances where the weight is evenly distributed on both feet tend to be stronger. If most of the weight is supported by one leg, the stability of the stance is lessened. Whatever the stance, once one foot leaves the ground, as when stepping or making a kicking attack, stability is reduced. These are all points to bear in mind when training for speed and considering when it might be appropriate to use footsweeps or other throwing techniques to down an opponent.

It is a good idea, especially for beginners, to dedicate some time to practising stances and learning how to link movements form one stance into another in different directions. Do not worry too much about performing strikes, blocks and kicks, just concentrate on the stances and ease of movement. Any given stance can be practised initially in four directions, to the front, and to the rear, and to the left and right sides. As expertise grows, it can be helpful to go 'around the clock' with given stances, imagining attackers coming in from different angles. Some styles consider there to be eight basic directions of attack, and others as many as fourteen. Forward and back stances are the main stances used in advancing and retreating. The majority of the exercises performed when doing five-step, three-step and one-step *kumite* rely on these stances, although many instructors will include sequences using *kiba-dachi* to practise side-kicks and back-kicks. One explanation sometimes given for the use of *kiba-dachi* is that it allows the karateka in a 'back to the wall' situation to kick to both sides and use his hands to deal with attackers coming in from the front.

*Fig 29    Stance practice should relate to actual combat. Assume the back stance as you block and be ready to...*

*Fig 30    ...switch to a forward stance as you counter-punch, rotating the hips as you thrust out the punching arm.*

Being able to switch from defence to offence as in the previous technique (Figs 29–30) is a very important skill. A quick, sudden attack may be blocked most effectively by drifting out of range using a back stance. In order to close with the opponent however it becomes necessary to switch through the rooted stance into the front stance. The untrained eye will scarcely even notice that the karateka has gone through the rooted stance phase, seeing just the back stance block and front stance counter punch.

Turning sideways on to an opponent reduces the target area as far as frontal direct attacks are concerned, but the possibility of being caught with hooking and roundhouse techniques may increase. Also, it is very dangerous to offer the unprotected side of the body to an opponent's direct attacks. In self defence terms the pectoral and abdominal muscles afford some measure of protection against attack, but there is very little muscle protecting the ribs and the spaces between them. A sideways stance also makes it easier for an attacker to kick to the kidneys, vulnerable organs in the lower back area which are virtually unprotected. In a competition scenario it is a good idea to know which techniques your opponent favours as this can determine the most effective stance to use for a given match, and which situations to avoid.

Sometimes, a fighter uses a stance to deliver a technique such as *kiba-dachi* to deliver a *yoko-geri* (side-kick), because the stance permits the kind of footwork necessary to get in range to deliver the kick. With *kiba-dachi* it is possible to cross-step to close the distance and get within kicking range, or to confuse the opponent and do *ushiro-geri* (back-kick) instead, when the opponent is prepared for the side kick.

## Correct Use of the Hips

The proper use of the hips is essential in all techniques and much of the impressive speed and power generated by karate experts is a result of getting the hips into the technique. The hip joints

*Fig 31   From a basic kiba-dachi stance where you are side on to your opponent there are numerous options for mounting an attack.*

are the largest in the body and they form the most important point of articulation of the body. The pelvis is the fulcrum linking the power of the legs and the back, connecting the thigh bones to the spinal column. Whether lifting, jumping, running or doing any other type of athletic movement the real power comes from, is coordinated by and is transmitted through, the hips. For most activities like walking and running we do not even think about the action of the hips because we learn the motor skills necessary to do these things in the early years of life.

The basic components of any technique are head, hips, hands and feet. The head's role is easy, it should be looking at the opponent for openings and signs of attack. The relative uses of hands and feet are determined by whether a block, kick or strike is to be used. In all cases the correct application of power through the hip action is vital.

*Fig 32   By making a cross step, placing the left leg in front of the right and transferring your weight on to your left foot you are well positioned to kick with the right leg, using either a side kick, yoko-geri or a roundhouse kick, mawashi-geri.*

*Fig 33   Alternatively, it is possible to pivot and position yourself to attack with a back kick, ushiro-geri. You can kick with either leg, depending on whether he tries to move in or out of range. It may be neccessary to make a short skipping step on the left foot.*

*Fig 34   The typical way of following up is to use ushiro-geri, the back kick, using the left foot to strike with.*

## Hip Rotation

Hip rotation, or hip turn, is vital to effective punching and blocking techniques. Power generated by the leg muscles, which are the biggest and strongest in the body, is transmitted into fast, snappy rotation of the hips, achieved by thrusting with the legs and twisting at the waist. The movement travels through the spine and assists the muscles of the upper body in the shoulders and chest to thrust out the fist at great speed. In a real sense, the body moves before the arm does, and the arm muscles themselves are kept relaxed until the moment of impact, when triceps, deltoids, forearm and wrist are tensed to make the punch more powerful, and faster.

The good strike has a whip-like quality, being thrust out and pulled back in a blur of fast action. The role of the abdominals and side oblique muscles in this is very important. This is one of the reasons why a lot of abdominal conditioning is done in most karate classes: it is not just done so that the abdomen will be well conditioned in order to receive blows. The rotation of the hips is at the core of karate training and must be studied and practised over and over again. While less showy and eye-catching than quick arm movements or high flashy kicks, time spent developing the proper hip action will pay dividends.

The most important points to remember are that the hips must be kept level, and the rotation must be continuous. When punching or blocking the shoulders should be turned simultaneously with the hips; the whole body must function as a single unit, and the body should be kept upright, rather than leaning forwards.

## Forward Thrust of the Hips

Thrusting the hips forward is of prime importance for developing fast, effective karate. The karateka has to be able to take big steps fearlessly in order to close distance, and driving the hips forward is a crucial component of this skill. A kick or punch in order to be deemed successful in contest, needs to be delivered with the thrust of the rear leg driving the hips into the technique. It is not sufficient just to step, the rear foot must push against the floor, propelling the body into the technique. The greater the thrust coming from the driving leg, the faster the body and, in turn, the block, punch or kick, will move. Hip thrust can be in a forwards, backwards or sideways direction.

Serious athletes and professional sportsmen are constantly re-examining the biomechanics of their favourite movements in order to perfect their technique, and martial artists must do exactly the same. The key to fluid, powerful, technically correct movements is continuous repetition of the basics. It is much better to do twenty repetitions of a movement such as *gyaku-zuki* and actually concentrate on correct form as you do each repetition than it is mindlessly and carelessly to do 200.

The correct use of stance and body positioning are the basis of proper training in karate, being perhaps the most important components in the successful application of many techniques.

## Exercises to Develop Hip Turn

There are various training methods to help develop kinesthetic awareness of the proper movement of the hips, or proprioception. By placing a broomstick across the small of the back and holding it in place the hips can be felt turning as a unit and it is easy to see if the hips are not level as the turn is performed by checking in a mirror. The basic drill to develop good hip turn is simple, but needs to be practised over and over again, because it is not an easy task to develop perfect hip rotation.

• Place the hands on the hips, the thumbs pointing inwards towards the backbone. Face forwards and hold the elbows out away from the body. Relax the shoulders and concentrate on the *tanden* area (the lower abdomen) as the centre of power in the body. Inhale, throwing the chest out without raising the shoulders and press the thumbs into the hip bones. Step forward into *hanmi*, the half front-facing position and, without altering the position of the feet or the knees and keeping the level of the hips constant, slowly turn the hips through 45 degrees to the side.

• The upper body will be rotated by the action of the hips. Turn your head so that you are facing forwards again and smoothly rotate the hips, keeping them level until the body is again facing forwards. As the movement is completed flex the rear leg and the muscles of the chest and abdominals.

• Once again, from *hanmi* rotate in the way just described, slowly and smoothly into the front-facing position and back again.

• As the movement becomes easier, gradually increase the speed and power of the rotation.

*Fig 35   Using a pole to check hip-turn.*

*Fig 36   The pole must turn without any vertical movement.*

# TURNING
## *(Figs 37 – 39)*

An important part of effective stance training is the development of a smooth, fast turn, so that the karateka, having dealt with an assailant facing him, can spin to face any threat that might be coming from the rear. The turning movement is usually practised from *zenkutsu-dachi*, when the class reach one end of the dojo while doing *kihon* in stepping punch for example. At the instructor's command of '*Mawate*' the rear leg slides across without the hips being twisted. When the foot reaches hip width on the other side of the body, the student spins on the balls of his feet, strongly twisting the hips by using a thrusting action of what was the bent, forward leg, and which now becomes the extended rear leg. Normally some blocking action such as *gedan-barai* is performed at the same time, and a '*kiai*' shout is made.

*Fig 37    Position just prior to making the turn.*

*Fig 38    The right leg slides across and the hips turn, pivoting on the balls of the feet as the arms cross ready to block.*

*Fig 39    As the turn and block are completed the left leg assists by adding thrust to the twisting of the hips.*

44

## *KIME* (FOCUS)

*Kime* is an important concept in karate training and fighting. Basically it is the ability to channel all the energy of a given movement into a strike, focusing it in the smallest possible area so that it is concentrated rather than dissipated. One famous karate teacher likened the development of *Kime* to the action of a hammer hitting a nail. A hammer hitting a thick block of wood does not penetrate, but merely dents the surface. This is because the broad area of the hammer head dissipates the energy of the strike. When the energy of the hammer is used instead to strike a nail it drives it deep into the wood. No more energy is used, but it is concentrated into a smaller area. This is the principle of *Kime*: the foot, or the fist, is the nail and the body is the hammer.

Two bedrock punching techniques, *oi-zuki* and *gyaku-zuki*, are frequently used to train correct stepping actions and to heighten awareness of the importance of proper stance and focus.

## *GYAKU-ZUKI* (REVERSE PUNCH)

The *gyaku-zuki* is perhaps the most important punching technique in karate. In competition it is by far the highest scoring technique. It is effective as a variable response technique in a variety of self defence situations and its mastery is the key to understanding many other karate techniques. It must be delivered from a strong stance and when done properly it generates a lot of force.

*Fig 40   Abdu Shaher, Lightweight World Champion, scoring with an accurate, focused gyaku-zuki.*

*Fig 41   A low gyaku-zuki attack by Mervyn Etienne on Mike Salisman. Dropping low can surprise an opponent, but if the knee touches the ground, some power is lost and the technique is less effective.*

### *Gyaku-zuki* **Basic Technique**
*(Figs 42–44)*

For the *gyaku-zuki* movement to be smooth and fast, the muscles must be relaxed, but, at the moment of impact, all the muscles should tense up and transmit the force of that sudden tension into the punch. The effective co-ordination of legs, hips, body arms and hands is not easy, and to perfect the technique requires long and dedicated practice.

Common faults include relying on the power of the arms and shoulders alone, not lowering the centre of gravity enough, not keeping the hips level, and failing to use the drive supplied by the rear leg to increase the effectiveness of the punch. Never close your eyes when punching; always look at your target and retain your awareness of his defences and any possible counters he may try.

*Fig 42    Starting in left hanmi with the right fist held at the right hip, the left arm is held out, extended in front of the body. The left hand is held open, with the finger tips in a line with the sternum.*

### *Gyaku-zuki* **Stepping Technique**
*(Figs 45–47)*

*Gyaku-zuki* should also be practised on the move. It is often practised after stepping back and blocking, but it also needs to be practised while advancing.

It is important to train with *Ma-ai*, or distance, always in mind. The lower or longer the final stance is, the greater the range of the *gyaku-zuki* will be. Resist the temptation to lean forwards when attacking with *gyaku-zuki*; it is better to take a longer step on the front foot, dropping the hips and lengthening the stance to reach the target. If you do this and still fail to reach the target, because of an adversary's speed or agility, immediately follow up with a *mae-geri* off the rear leg. Do not take such a long step and get so low when trying the punch that you lose spring and cannot move easily when you have to.

*Fig 45    Starting from left hanmi. Punch with the right arm, so that the right arm and left leg are advanced, then...*

*Fig 43   The punch is delivered starting from hanmi and finishing in zenkutsu-dachi, with a snappy rotation of the hips, which should be kept level throughout the movement.*

*Fig 44   As the hips turn, the front leg pulls the hip round as the rear leg flexes, pushing down and into the ground. The left hand is pulled back to the left hip as the right arm straightens at the elbow.*

*Fig 46   ...take a step bringing the right (rear) leg through in a semi-circular gliding movement so that the feet almost come together and the knees almost touch. Narrowing the stance as the step is made is very important for self protection and speed. Making the step with the feet shoulder width apart leaves the groin  vulnerable to a kicking attack.*

*Fig 47   Slide the right foot out in front, ending in right zenkutsu-dachi as the hips rotate and the left arm punches through.The right arm bends at the elbow and the right hand is pulled in to the hip as the left elbow locks out straight, the fist rotating so that the palm faces the floor. Concentrate the force of the strike into the two large knuckles of the left fist.*

47

## Reverse Punch –Tips
*(Fig 47a)*

• Many people, as they perform the *gyaku-zuki* movement, have a tendency to raise their hips. This should be avoided.

• Keep the hips low and grip the floor with the soles of the feet.

• Pay attention too to the line taken by the elbow as you punch. There is often a tendency for the elbow to creep out, which results in a loss of speed and power. The elbow of the punching hand should lightly brush against the side of the body as you punch.

• Putting too much shoulder into the punch or leaning forward will mean that the power generated by the hip rotation is dissipated. Try to keep the shoulder relaxed and deliver the blow with the energy generated by the hip rotation alone.

• The quicker and sharper the hip turn, the better the technique will be.

## OI-ZUKI (STEPPING PUNCH)
### (Fig 48)

*Oi-zuki* is a direct-attack stepping punch. It is sometimes called the lunge punch, and its practice is of fundamental importance to anyone who really wants to improve in karate. Many people are attracted to the spectacular kicking techniques and the esoteric aspects of *kata*, but proper attention to basics is the real way to develop expert levels of skill and deep understanding of karate technique. Continuous repetitive practice of *oi-zuki* develops the ability to cover ground fast and decisively to get in range to strike the opponent. The power and speed of the step has to be transmitted into the punch in one smooth, fluid, focused movement. Much time is spent going up and down the dojo, practising this technique and the *gyaku-zuki*, but it is important not to become lax. Many *kyu* grades do not really understand the value of practice. They have the attitude that they already know the technique and would rather practise something new, different or more exciting. As a result they do not put 100 per cent into the training, but rather go through the motions until they get to the bits they find interesting! Even when every step and punch is not performed at full speed and power they should be done with full concentration on the movement.

*Fig 48   Middleweight World Champion Masci of France on the attack with oi-zuki.*

## *Oi-zuki* (Stepping Punch)

*(Figs 49 – 51)*

This technique must be practised right and left, the aim being to make both left and right hand punches equally fast and correct.

Theoretically, it is possible to generate more power by leaning the body into the strike so that the supporting leg and punching arm thrust in opposite directions along the same plane. This action is favoured by Shukokai stylists, but in Shorin styles, Shotokan and Wado-Ryu, the body is kept upright, sacrificing the slight extra power gain for the sake of stability and a posture which allows the karateka to move easily into the next technique.

*Fig 49   Oi-zuki is a large movement. Step forward rapidly from left zenkutsu-dachi, holding the right hand at the side of the body just above the hip, and drawing the foot in close to the left, supporting, foot as you step. The right foot describes a shallow semi-circle, passing close to the supporting foot.*

*Fig 52   The shukokai version of oi-zuki, theoretically more powerful, but more committed than in the Shotokan method.*

*Fig 50    It continues sliding lightly over the floor and moving out to the width of the hips as it advances. During this movement the hips have moved forward and the left leg supports all the weight of the body throughout the stepping action. Its function switches from load bearing to thrust as the hips continue to drive forwards and...*

*Fig 51    ...the weight of the body is partially transferred to the front foot. The front knee bends as the hips thrust forward, and the arm straightens, punching out the fist with all the energy of the stepping body transmitted into the fist.*

*Fig 53    Correct finishing position for oi-zuki in the Shotokan style.*

# BLOCKING BASICS

Stepping quickly, using *zenkutsu-dachi* as the base for generating speed and power as well as being vital to making effective punching attacks, is also a key component of many blocking actions. Blocks may not be as spectacular as the striking techniques, the knife hands and roundhouse kicks, but they are essential for self defence. All true *kata* begin with a blocking movement, indicating the essentially defensive nature of karate. Training in blocking improves students' understanding of timing and distance and develops confidence in their ability to read an opponent's intentions and to defend themselves. There is a considerable variety of blocking techniques which combine with various body movements and evasions to provide a defence against virtually any type of unarmed attack.

Blocks are discussed in more detail in chapters three and four, but the aim at this point is to show how the execution of an effective block is determined by the correct use of stance and footwork. Blocks can be made stepping forwards or backwards or while side-stepping. A block made stepping forwards is more powerful than when done stepping backwards, but the karateka has less time to do it in. Stepping backwards and blocking is a little easier, because it combines blocking with evasion and gives the karateka more time to block and counter than he has when stepping forward to block an incoming attack. Consequently blocking as you step back may be more useful when faced with quicker, more agile opponents whom it may not be possible to block

by stepping forwards to meet their incoming attack. Stepping forwards to block requires surer timing and accurate judgment of distance, courage and decisiveness. If already in a free-fighting situation the defender may decide not to step forwards or backwards when blocking, but remain planted and concentrate on a solid block and counter.

## *Jodan age uke* (Rising Block)
*(Figs 54 – 55)*

The rising block is used principally to defend against punching attacks to the face, although it can be used to defend against head-height kicks and clubbing attacks with sticks or truncheon-like weapons.

The defender is in left free-fighting *kamae* and the attacker steps in to attack with *jodan oi-zuki* (stepping punch to the face). The rising block is made by lifting the forearm and contacting just under the attacker's wrist. Note how the right hand is pulled back to the right hip ready to counter and to add hip twist to the blocking action. Note also how the knee of the defender's front leg bends and the back leg straightens into *zenkutsu-dachi* transferring the power of the legs and hips into the blocking action of the arm. This is one of the principles that makes karate techniques so powerful: the use of the whole body, not just the arm, when making a block or a punch. If the block were attempted simply by lifting the arm, it would probably lack the power to deflect the punch and the defender would be likely to get hit in the face.

*Fig 54*

*Fig 55*

*Fig 56   A jumping backfist or uraken to the head scores spectacularly in a semi-contact bout.*

# 3 Upper Body Techniques

*'The way of the martial arts begins after 1,000 days study and after 10,000 days we may begin to learn the meaning of karate.'*
Oyama Matsutatsu

In traditional styles of karate the hands and feet are the principal weapons used by the karateka for fighting. The legs, while up to four times more powerful than the hands, are both slower and more difficult to use for striking, especially when the head is the target, so all forms of karate give great importance to punching and other strikes delivered with different parts of the hand. In traditional schools the hands were hardened and strengthened by using a variety of conditioning methods to turn them into deadly weapons. The old teachers on Okinawa used to say that the fingers must become knives, the finger tips arrowheads, and the edges of the hands, swords and spears. The *makiwara*, or punching post, was the most commonly used device for hardening the hands. By striking it thousands of times students could form calluses on otherwise soft parts of their hands, making them as tough as leather. The effect of being struck by a conditioned hand is akin to being hit with a wooden club or bludgeon. Once conditioned, the hand not only does more damage to the target, but it is also less likely to be injured by concussive contact with hard bony parts of the body, such as the skull. It is important to understand that it is not just the fact that the hand itself that is harder which makes the techniques so devastating, but that it is the whole network of connective tissue, ligaments, tendons and muscles that are strengthened by the *makiwara* training process. The wrists, elbows, hips and shoulders all play their part in delivering the power that is focused in the fist; likewise the toes, knees and ankles do the same when kicking.

## MAKING A FIST
*(Fig 57)*

The forefist is the principal weapon of most karate schools and the first thing trainees must learn is how to make a proper fist. The basic method is as follows:
• Straighten the hand, extending the fingers fully.
• Bend the fingers at the first and second (middle) knuckle joints until the finger tips touch the fleshy pads at the base of the fingers.
• Bend from the main large knuckles, making the fist into a tight ball.
• Curl the thumb over the index and middle fingers and grip tightly to make a solid, firm fist.

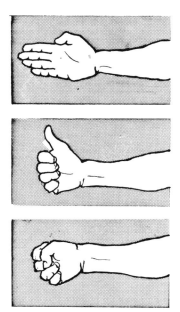

*Fig 57   Making a fist.*

*Fig 58   Seiken, the forefist.*

It is important to remember to squeeze with the outside edge of the hand when forming a fist in this way as the little finger tends to relax and may be injured when delivering punches or blocking kicks if you forget to concentrate on keeping it tightly tucked in. After constant practice the fist can be formed very quickly.

Another method, less popular now, but which was used a lot in the past, involved bending the bottom three fingers of the hand first then folding the index finger over at a slight angle to the middle finger, keeping the index finger extended rather than bent at the final joint. The thumb is then curled over the top, pressing the index finger into the muscular base of the thumb. This method keeps the first two fingers tightly locked in position, but the lazy and little fingers may tend to uncurl, weakening the overall strength of the fist if the karateka forgets to concentrate on keeping them tight.

## *Seiken* (Forefist)
*(Fig 58)*

The forefist is the blow most used in karate, so it is important that it is practised assiduously. It is the point of delivery for all the major *tsuki* (strikes) such as *oi-zuki*, and *gyaku-zuki* which were describe in the previous chapter. The striking area should be that covered by the two largest knuckles of the hand; those of the index and middle fingers. At the point of impact, the wrist and these knuckles must form a straight line, as power is dissipated if the wrist is bent and there is a risk of injury to the joint. The whole power of the body must be transmitted through the arm into the fist. The wrist elbow and shoulder rotate in a corkscrewing action as the fist travels to the target. Because it is a strong weapon, the forefist can be used against hard or soft parts of the body and is usually used to strike the abdomen and thorax, as well as the face.

*Fig 59   Correct punching technique, demonstrated by the European Kata champion, Marcini of Italy.*

## *Choku-zuki* (**Straight Punch**)

*Choku-zuki* is the basis of techniques like *oi-zuki* and *gyaku-zuki*. It is a punching movement used to train the karateka in the correct use of the muscles of the torso and upper body when punching.

### Technique

*(Figs 60–64)*

*Choku-zuki* is normally practised in a natural body position with the feet held at shoulder width apart and the hips square to the front.

• The punch must travel in a straight line to the target, with the shoulders being kept in a relaxed and natural position.

• The upper body should be kept perpendicular to the ground. Avoid leaning forwards or backwards.

• The elbows should stay in close to the body line. If you raise one shoulder this will cause the elbow to go out to the side.

• The hand which is pulled back to the hip should travel just as fast as the hand being punched out to the target. The faster you pull back the leading arm, the more speed and power will be transmitted into your punch.

• Remember to tense the abdominal muscles properly upon focusing each punch and remember to relax before beginning the next punch.

• Some students find it helpful to open the fist after completing each punch, as a reminder to relax before beginning the next one. If this is helpful, particularly with beginners, then use it, but with more experienced karateka it should not really be necessary.

Fig 60   The left arm is extended, with the fist clenched and the palm facing down, the two striking knuckles being in a line with the sternum. The shoulders must be in a straight line and square on to an imaginary opponent, and the right fist is held touching the body just above the right hip.

Fig 63   As the right arm straightens the left fist comes to rest just above the left hip.

Fig 61    *The left hand is pulled back towards the hip at the same time as the right hand is pushed out.*

Fig 62    *The left fist twists and passes the right fist as it rotates in the opposite direction, twisting through 180 degrees.*

Fig 64    *The right arm is extended, palm downwards, and the fist maintained at chest height in a line with the sternum.*

## ZUKI (PUNCHING TECHNIQUES)

*Gyaku-zuki* and *oi-zuki* which were described fully in the previous chapter, are the two main punching movements in karate, but by no means the only ones. There is a variety of other punches that can be used depending on how many opponents you face, how close or far away an adversary is, whether he is stationary or coming in to the attack, whether he is positioned in front, behind or to the side of you, whether he is taller or shorter than you, and so on.

Common training drills involve *ren-zuki*, cluster punching done using both hands, usually in twos and threes, and *dan-zuki*, repetition punching with the same hand, again usually done in quick succession for no more than three consecutive punches. Finally there is a group of punches done using both hands simultaneously called *morote-zuki*. These are advanced techniques best studied seriously by higher grades.

## *Kizami-zuki* (Jab)

*(Figs 65–67)*

*Kizami-zuki* is a jabbing punch done off the leading hand. Power comes from the rear leg thrusting and from the rotation of the hips, so as the left hand pistons out, the left hip makes a small twist as the right leg pushes. The hips should rotate fast and the right hand must pull back to the hip to add force to the jab. The jab can be an effective knockout punch in its own right, but it is normally used as a lead in to combinations, and will often precede a decisive attack with a reverse or lunge punch. Depending on how an opponent blocks or evades the jab he can be set up for a variety of effective combinations. Often, the jab is done without stepping forward or moving the front leg, as this tends to telegraph the punch, so it is important to develop a good sense of distance and proper timing.

*Fig 65*

## *Nagashi-zuki* (Floating Punch)

*(Figs 68–71)*

Similar in feeling to the lunge punch, this one is done on a 45-degree diagonal, either moving forwards or backwards, or simply pivoting on the front foot. It is used as a counter-attack, by sidestepping an opponent and hitting him in passing, or as a direct attack anticipating and avoiding his counter with body evasion. The opponent attacks with a lunge punch which the defender sidesteps, blocking with *soto-uke* as he slips his counterpunch over the extended arm, striking his opponent in the jaw.

*Fig 68*

Fig 66

Fig 67

Fig 69

Fig 70

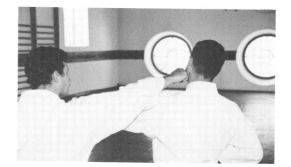

Fig 71

### *Tate-zuki* (Vertical Fist)

(Figs 72–73)

*Tate-zuki* is perhaps better understood as a fist position than as a different kind of punch. The punching action is the same as for *choku-zuki*, but the finishing position of the fist, which is determined by the distance of the opponent from the person doing the strike, and by the target area, is horizontal rather than vertical. From the normal, fully extended *seiken* position, the fist is turned clockwise through 90 degrees, a quarter turn of the wrist.

*Fig 72*

### *Ura-zuki* (Close Punch)

(Figs 74–77)

*Ura-zuki* is a punch delivered with the palm facing upwards at close range. It can be used to attack the body, particularly the solar plexus and ribs. At very close range it can function as an upper-cut to the jaw.

*Fig 73*

*Fig 74*

*Fig 75*

*Fig 76*

*Fig 77*

### *Kagi-zuki* (**Hook Punch**)
*(Fig 78)*

*Kagi-zuki* is a hook punch delivered with the elbow bent at 90 degrees. It is usually used after side-stepping to attack the sides of the opponent's body, landing under the ribs, but can be used to the solar plexus. It is very important to tense the muscles of the sides and back when punching.

### *Mawashi-zuki* (**roundhouse**)
*(Fig 79)*

The roundhouse punch is delivered with the wrist twisted in a three-quarters turn from the starting position. The thumb should be facing downwards as the fist lands. It is a straight punch which turns into a sort of hook, since the elbow is kept into the side until the last possible moment. The punch is delivered with a twisting motion of the hip. It is usually done with the basic forefist.

## *MOROTE-ZUKI* (**TWO-HANDED PUNCHES**)

These are advanced techniques requiring correct body movement and co-ordination to be effective. They combine speed and a double threat. *Morote-zuki* are not common, but an opponent has twice as much difficulty in blocking two punches as he would have blocking one.

### *Awase-zuki* (**U Punch**)
*(Fig 80)*

The U punch is done to the opponent's front and the intention is to attack with both fists simultaneously, usually striking the head and body. Here one hand does a reverse punch to the heart, as the other attacks the liver, the back of the hand facing down as in *ura-zuki*.

### *Yama-zuki* (**Wide U Punch**)
*(Fig 81)*

This wider version of the U punch is used to attack the lower abdomen or groin and the throat or face simultaneously. The hands are held further apart than in the U punch and the shoulder of the upper arm is raised higher.

*Fig 78*

*Fig 79*

*Fig 80*

*Fig 81*

### *Heiko-zuki* (**Parallel Punch**)

*(Fig 82)*

This is a double straight punch, targeting the ribs under the pectorals or the floating ribs, using either forefist or extended knuckle strikes. Both fists are held on the hips, and, from *zenkutsu-dachi* punched out simultaneously forwards. It is vital to extend the rear leg to generate effective power.

### *Hasami-zuki* (**Scissors Punch**)

*(Figs 83 – 84)*

The scissors punch is done from a natural posture, *kiba-dachi* or *zenkutsu-dachi*. The fists describe a semi-circle from the starting position on the hips, striking *seiken* or extended knuckle to either the sides of the body, the neck or the face. This technique, slightly modified by using bear hand or cupping the palms, is sometimes shown as a defence against a frontal bear hug under the arms. The ears are attacked and if done with sufficient force ear drum damage can result. Great care must be taken practising such techniques in the dojo as it is all too easy to injure a training partner unintentionally.

Fig 82

Fig 83

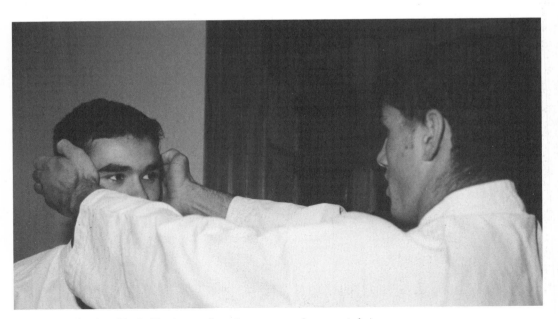

*Fig 84   Bear hand combined with scissors strike to the ears, a very dangerous technique.*

## *URAKEN* (BACKFIST)

*(Fig 85)*

The backfist is used to strike the face and head, and sometimes the side of the thoracic cavity. It is formed in exactly the same way as the forefist but the striking area is the top of the two large knuckles and the back of the hand. The backfist is a very quick technique that should be delivered with a whiplash, snapping motion of the arm.

The backfist can be delivered vertically or horizontally. It can be used as a direct attack, as a range finder or as a stunning technique in its own right. It is relatively easy to do, enjoying equal popularity in full contact and semi-contact and has numerous self defence applications. To score in competition, the blow has to be delivered from a recognized stance. Jumping backfists sometimes score, depending on whether the referee feels skill and good timing has been shown.

### Vertical Backfist

The vertical attack is usually delivered from a free-fighting stance, using the front hand. The attacker in right stance closes the distance by stepping in to his opponent, making a half step forwards on his on his right foot. As he does so, he brings his rear foot up close behind his front foot and simultaneously raises and crosses his arms. He switches his weight and drops into a back stance as he delivers the blow, whipping the right

*Fig 85 Backfist strike to the jaw*

hand out in a downwards arc, and pulling the left fist back to his side just above his hip. This is a powerful strike, not just a flick of the wrist.

### Horizontal Backfist

*(Fig 86)*

The horizontal backfist is used in competition, like the jab in boxing, as an attack to the face off the lead hand, or as the first punch in a combination. It is a more versatile punch than a jab, and is useful in self defence situations where attacks do not always come from the front. It is also used as a counter, sometimes combining the strike with a trapping block, grabbing the opponent's sleeve so that he cannot move away from the blow.

*Fig 86 Horizontal backfist strike to the temple.*

## *Kentsui* (Hammerfist or Bottomfist)
*(Fig 87)*

Also known as *Tetsui* (iron hammer) and *shutsui* (hand hammer). The muscular bottom edge of the hand is used like a hammer to strike areas such as the collar-bone, nose or even the top of the head. This seemingly crude technique can generate great destructive force and can be used most effectively to attack the face in a ground fighting situation should the karateka be knocked off his feet.

*Fig 87 Ketsui or tetsui, the iron hammer fist.*

## *Ippon Ken* (Extended Knuckle Fist)
*(Fig 88)*

By forming the forefist but extending the knuckle of the index finger and pressing down on it to strengthen it, it is possible to focus considerable energy into a very small area. This technique can be used to attack the bridge of the nose, the philtrum and the weak points between the ribs. It can be used in any situation where a forefist strike using *oi-zuki*, *gyaku-zuki* or any of the other major punches is appropriate.

*Fig 88   Ippon ken, the extended knuckle fist.*

## *Nakadaka-ken* (Middle Finger Extended Knuckle Fist)
*(Fig 89)*

This is a similar technique to *ippon ken*, but instead of using the protruding index finger, the middle finger protrudes. This fist is formed by squeezing the index and ring fingers together and folding the thumb over the index and middle finger and pressing down tightly.

*Fig 89   Nakadaka ken, the middle finger knuckle strike.*

## *Hiraken* (Fore Knuckle Fist)
*(Fig 90)*

*Hiraken* is formed by bending the fingers until the tips are touching the fleshy pads on the palms of the hand and pressing the thumb forcefully in to the side of the hand. This position is half-way between the open-handed *shuto* and the forefist (*seiken*). It is used to attack the point under the nose, just above the mouth, or the throat or the weak points between the ribs. It increases the karateka's striking range by 2–5 cm (1-2in).

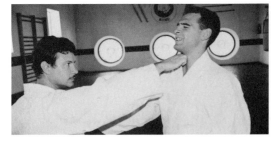

*Fig 90   Hiraken, the fore knuckle fist.*

## KAISHO (OPEN HAND STRIKES)

*Kaisho*, or open hand techniques, are done by extending the fingers and pressing them tightly together. The thumb should be bent and pressed in tightly against the side of the palm of the hand. The hand can then be used after the fashion of a knife, sword or spear, depending on whether you strike with the edge (side of hand) or point (fingertips).

### Haishu (Backhand)
*(Fig 91)*

The open handed backhand is mainly used for blocking, but its efficacy as a striking technique is often underestimated. It can be used to strike the face, solar plexus or sides of the body with considerable effect.

### Nukite (Spear Hand)
*(Fig 92)*

The spear hand is only ever used for self defence purposes. It is a difficult technique to perfect, requiring lots of practice, but extremely valuable for self defence. The extended fingers increase the range of a striking technique by 10–12cm (4 – 5 inches), depending on the length of the fingers.

The middle finger is bent so that the tips of the index, middle and ring fingers form the striking point. This blow is used against soft body parts like the solar plexus, and also to attack the bridge of the nose and the eyes. A light jabbing action with the tips of the fingers to the nose or to either eye is extremely disconcerting, as the eyes are the most vulnerable organs of the body. Even partial contact is enough to obscure the vision temporarily, leaving an attacker blind to follow-up techniques. Great care is necessary in training and practice as serious eye injury can easily result.

### Nihon Nukite (Two Point Spear Hand)
*(Fig 93)*

This is a variation, where the index and middle fingers are used to strike into the eyes themselves, is only justifiable in life-threatening situations.

Fig 91    Haishu, the backhand strike.

Fig 92    Nukite or spear hand is a very important self defence technique.

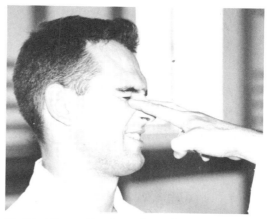

Fig 93    Nihon nukite, the two fingered strike to the eyes.

## *Teisho* (Palm Heel)

*(Fig 94)*

The palm heel is another traditional karate weapon used for self defence which is not used in competition. It can be used to strike the sternum, solar plexus, jaw and nose. It is a simple technique for beginners and those who have difficulty in making a tight fist. It is important to strike with a rapid, explosive movement, as there is a tendency, especially among lower grades, to turn it into a pushing movement. It has the advantage over punching attacks to the nose in as much as the risk of hand damage is minimized because there is less likelihood of accidentally striking the teeth than there is when punching.

Fig 94   Teisho, the palm heel strike.

## *Shuto* (Knife Hand)

*(Fig 95)*

Often called *te-gatana* or hand sword by the old ju-jitsu schools, the *shuto* is to many the epitome of the karate technique. Often referred to by the uninitiated as the 'karate chop' it is an extremely elegant and precise technique that allows the karateka to perform blocking or striking movements with great focus and precision. Although the hand is kept open, it is never held in relaxed fashion as this invites injury. Tension must be maintained in the hand, the fingers have to be pressed together and the thumb folded into the palm at the base of the index finger. Suitable and popular targets include the side of the neck, back of the neck, collarbones, back of the elbow (when the attacker's arm is extended) and the ribs.

Fig 95   Shuto, the knife hand strike, better known to the uninitiated as the karate chop.

## *Seiryuto* (Ox-jaw hand)

*(Fig 96)*

A variant of the palm heel strike is the ox-jaw hand. This involves forming a *shuto* or knife hand and bending the wrist, and using the bottom edge of the hand as the striking area. This curved hand can be used to make clubbing attacks to the face and collar bones.

Fig 96   Seiryuto, the ox-jaw hand strike, being used here to strike the collar bone.

## *Haito* (Ridge Hand)
*(Fig 97)*

The ridge hand is formed just like the knife hand, but the striking area used to deliver the blow is the opposite side of the hand to the knife hand: the striking area is the part of the hand where the outside edge of the index finger joins with the thumb. Targets are the same as for the knife hand, but this technique is delivered in a different way which allows for its application in different situations. The delivery action is almost like throwing a discus and great force can be generated even at close range. Because the action is the reverse of that performed in a *shuto* strike it is very important not to let the arm straighten or over-extend as it is easy to jar the elbow joint. Always keep a slight bend in the arm, so that the muscles and bones absorb the shock, rather than the ligaments around the elbow.

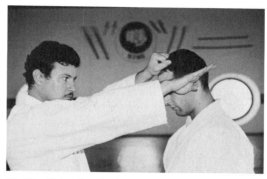

*Fig 97    Haito, the ridge hand, combined with a hair grab.*

## RARE HAND TECHNIQUES

## *Kakuto* (Bent Wrist)
*(Fig 98)*

*Kakuto* is primarily used as a striking block, using the back of the wrist against an opponent's punching arm, but can be used against the jaw, face and sometimes the armpit.

*Fig 98    Kakuto, the bent wrist strike.*

## *Keito* (Chicken Head Wrist)
*(Fig 99)*

The hand is bent in the opposite direction to that in the ox-jaw, and the fingers and thumb are flexed slightly inwards. The base and first joint of the thumb are used to block and strike with.

*Fig 99    Keito, chicken head strike.*

# ATE-WAZA (SMASHING TECHNIQUES)

## *Empi* (Elbows)

The elbows are extremely powerful weapons, and can be devastatingly effective in close-range self defence situations. Strictly speaking they are, together with knee strikes, classed as *ate-waza* (smashing techniques), but they are usually described within the general category of *uchi* (striking). Elbow strikes are not allowed in normal karate competition as they are difficult to control and dangerous. In semi-contact style fighting, the problem of distance would also make them difficult techniques to land. From a self defence point of view they are very useful, as even beginners, after a little training, are capable of generating enough power with elbow strikes to be able to break boards. Primarily close-range weapons, women and children can use them generate enough power to hurt an adult male assailant after a short amount of training.

Elbow strikes can be used to the front, the side or the rear with ease. They should never be used with full power against the vital points of the body, as serious damage or death can result. Techniques such as the reverse elbow strike to the temple can easily cause serious injury or death. Any elbow strikes aimed at the head will cause considerable damage, and can only be justified in extreme situations as a last resort.

Muay Thai, a form of full-contact kick boxing, allows full power blows with both elbows and knees to the face and head, and these techniques have caused a number of fatalities. Even glancing, hooking elbow strikes hitting a non-vital target like the forehead can cause wounds requiring ten to twenty stitches. It is always as well to bear in mind the probable result of actually delivering techniques in a real situation.

The advantage the elbow strike affords is that it allows relatively weak people to strike with enough focus and energy to knock out a much bigger, stronger aggressor if necessary, with little danger of hurting themselves. The jaw is the main target area in such cases.

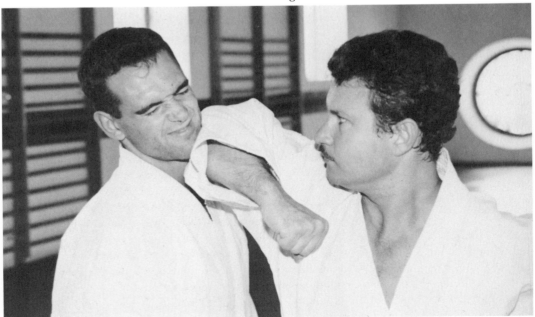

*Fig 100   The basic front elbow strike, mae-hiji-ate, a devastatingly powerful close range weapon.*

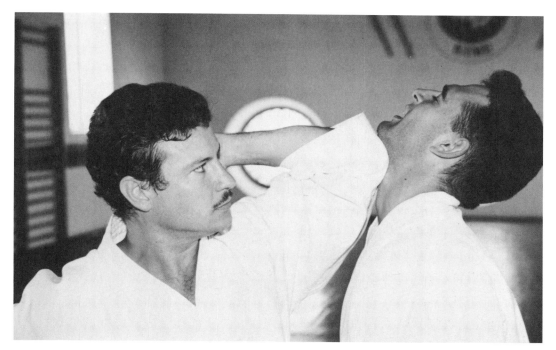

*Fig 101    Tate-hiji-ate, the upper-cut elbow strike, is extremely effective when used at close range to attack the jaw. Because it is relatively easy to generate great force with little risk of inury, elbow strikes are often used by beginners to demonstrate breaking techniques.*

## *Mae-hiji-ate* (Basic Front Elbow Strike)

*(Fig 100)*

This is a frontal attack, also known as *mae-empi-uchi*, which can be delivered as a hooking or crossing movement and is supremely effective when fighting at close range. The point of the chin, the side of the jaw and the nose are all valid targets. The chin and jaw are potential knock-out blows and the nose strike causes considerable pain and bleeding, and has a stunning and disconcerting effect on the person hit. It is delivered from a free-fighting stance and power is generated by making a similar hip action to that used in the reverse punch. If used with a side step it can also be delivered in a *kiba-dachi* stance.

## *Tate-hiji-ate* (Front Upper-Cut Elbow Strike)

*(Fig 101)*

This technique, also called *Tate-empi-uchi*, and can be delivered very effectively against an attacker as he comes in to attack. It is very important to bend the legs at the knees and use the power generated by straightening them in conjunction with the turning of the hips and the lifting of the elbow. Pull the opposite fist back to the hip as the elbow strike is made, in preparation to following up and in order to increase the power of the hip turn. The cleft of the chin or the point of the jaw should be the target areas.

### *Yoko-hiji-ate* (Side Elbow Strike)
*(Fig 102)*

This technique is also known as *yoko-empi-uchi* and can be used when an attacker comes in from the side. The normal target areas are the jaw, the solar plexus, the floating ribs, the liver or the heart area. Again, the defender first drops into a strong horse or straddle stance, to ensure that he has a solid base from which to strike his attacker, and the left fist is pulled back to the hip for a possible follow up.

It is also an easy matter to follow up with a vertical back fist to the face, or a knife hand to the groin, using the right hand immediately after the elbow strike. These techniques delivered in this situation will lack power but can be very quick and have a stunning, disorientating effect if the elbow strike fails to wind or knock down the attacker.

*Fig 102   Side elbow strike to the solar plexus.*

### *Ushiro-hiji-ate* (Back Elbow Strike)
*(Fig 103)*

The basic back elbow strike is sometimes called *ushiro-empi-uchi* and is used when an attacker approaches from the rear, attempting any kind of grabbing or grappling attack. As the attacker moves in, the defender extends his arm in front of him and then dropping his hips into a *kiba-dachi* horse stance, drives it back into his attacker's solar plexus, taking care to keep the elbow in close to the body so that power is not lost. If necessary, the other hand can be used to augment the power of the elbow strike, by pressing the palm against the fist of the striking arm.

*Fig 103   A hand-assisted back elbow strike to the ribs.*

### *Otoshi-hiji-ate* (**Downwards Elbow Strike**)
*(Figs 104–105)*

This technique, which is also know as *otoshi-empi-uchi*, can be used either by jumping up above the opponent and driving the elbow downwards into the head, nose or collarbone; or when the opponent is in a bent-over position with the head down (as when a boxer bores in to attack the midsection with body punches, or someone with rugby experience goes to grab the legs intending to tackle his intended victim to the ground). The opponent can be forced into this compromised position by grabbing his hair and pulling his head down, exposing the back of the neck and base of the skull which are vulnerable target areas. Alternatively an arm lock with a twist can be used, and the extended straight arm can be attacked by striking the elbow joint in the straight, extended position, which will at the very least cause ligament damage, and may dislocate the joint, causing nerve, muscle and ligament damage; again, a potentially crippling technique.

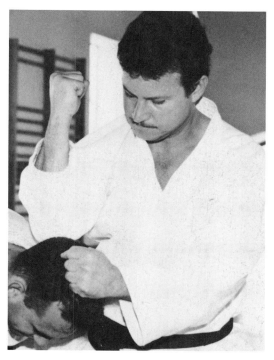

*Fig 104    Downwards elbow strike to the nape of the neck.*

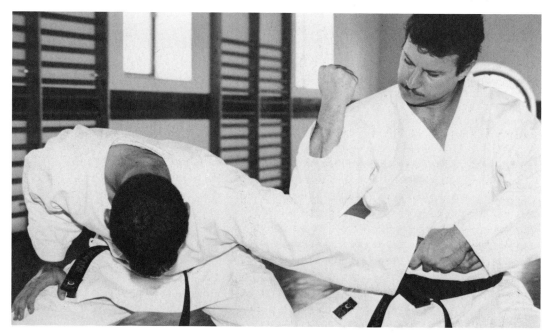

*Fig 105    Downwards elbow strike to the opponent's extended elbow joint.*

### *Mawari-yoko-hiji-ate* (Spinning Side Elbow)

*(Figs 106–108)*

This technique is done by trapping the attacker's outstretched arm as he punches. The defender adopts a back stance and makes an inside block, then hooks the blocking arm over the attacker's extended arm and spins through 180 degrees, pivoting on his right foot as he does so, and stepping behind and to the side of the attacker. This action painfully locks the outstretched punching arm at the elbow and helps prevent the attacker from moving out of range or even ducking. Using the rotational force generated by stepping and turning the defender can slam an elbow strike into the attacker's back, the kidneys, the side of the jaw or the ear – the choice of target area probably being determined by the relative heights of both individuals and the amount of damage the defender wishes, or needs, to inflict.

*Fig 106    Starting position, both fighters are same sided.*

*Fig 107    As the attacker's arm straightens, pivot and hook..*

*Fig 108    ...the arm, spinning in behind the attacker with a back elbow strike.*

*Fig 109    Soto-uke, the outer block; detail of arm action.*

## *UKE* (BLOCKING)

As karate is a defensive art, good blocking is of crucial importance. The first principle of blocking is to ensure that the opponent's attack does not hit its target, the second is to prepare the counter-attack. Blocks can be made using many of the hand positions already described, such as the palm heel or knife hand, but the most common blocks are performed with closed fists, the forearms or wrists being the contact areas used to focus the block. Some hard styles of karate devote a fair amount of time to conditioning in pairs, banging the insides and outsides of the forearms against each other repeatedly to toughen them up for the demands of hard contact and solid blocking techniques. Others prefer a softer approach, relying on technique and skilful twisting movements of the wrists and forearms to augment the deflecting qualities of their blocks.

Blocks can differ dramatically in force and effectiveness, depending upon the requirements of a given situation. An attack can be blocked with just enough force to parry or deflect the attack, allowing you to move to a safe distance and wait to see if further attacks will take place. Alternatively, a block can be delivered with enough force to cause considerable pain and even injury, discouraging further attack. Blocks can be used to knock the opponent off balance, or to turn him, exposing vulnerable areas such as the back, neck and kidneys. They can also be used to open up the opponent for a subsequent counter-attack, exposing vital target areas. The blocking action can be performed simultaneously with the counter-attack and can be used to pre-empt an opponent's attack, although this requires a high degree of anticipation on the part of the blocker. Blocks can be performed against both punching and kicking attacks.

There are many anecdotes about old masters of karate whose blocks were so powerful and painful to any would-be attackers that they did not need to use direct attacking techniques to defend themselves. A solid block could temporarily paralyse an arm or a leg, discouraging all thought of subsequent attacks. Many students of karate today train with a strong emphasis on contest, where generally fast, light blocking is called for, and tend to concentrate on continuous attacking combinations. In real combat effective defence depends on good blocking. Really good blocking, in a self defence situation, as has already been indicated, may even pre-empt the need to make an overtly aggressive strike at an assailant.

## Types of Block

In any blocking technique the most important thing is to judge correctly the trajectory of the opponent's technique. The block is then used to alter that trajectory.

There are four basic blocks which use the wrists and forearms to catch and deflect the opponents' attacks. These are *jodan age-uke*: the rising block, which is used against attacks aimed at the face and head; *Soto-uke* (outer block) and *uchi-uke* (inner block), which are both used against attacks aimed at the midsection, throat and jaw; and *gedan-barai*, which is used to defend against attacks aimed anywhere from the waist down. These four are the core blocking techniques of most styles of karate, and should be practised until they are fully automatic responses to attack.

Other blocking techniques include knife hands, which often combine block and counter attack, and augmented blocks, where two arms are used to strengthen the block against particularly powerful attacks. The X-block is an augmented block which is often used against powerful front kick attacks aimed at the groin. Trapping blocks involve catching an extended arm or leg before it can be pulled back and often precede a counter involving a footsweep or throw. Scooping blocks function in much the same way, typically being used against kicks to unbalance the attacker, setting him up for an effective counter. Pressing, hooking and sweeping blocks also exist and normally fall into one or other of the categories mentioned above. Most of the following blocks when practised in training involve making large movements which initially strike the beginner as being long and slow. Many advanced fighters shorten the blocking movements considerably when sparring, but the beginner must resist the temptation to do the same in practising *kumite*. Advanced karateka have much better co-ordination, and can generate considerable power with smaller movements, but most movements tend to shorten and become smaller under the stress of actual combat as we try to make them faster. Making the full movement in training means that the trainee is more likely to reproduce something approaching correct technique in combat. Shortening and skimping on movements in basic training will lead to them becoming ineffective in combat. It is equally important not to lengthen the blocking movements beyond their optimum position: moving the arm too far away from the body, over-turning the hips and so on, will all lead to a loss of balance.

*Fig 110    The arm action in shuto-uke, knife hand block.*

*Fig 111    Under the pressure of competition, good blocking form often deteriorates and combatants attempt to stop techniques any way that they can. Here the left knee lifting and both arms waving around combine to create a not very aesthetically pleasing, but nonetheless effective, defence.*

## *Jodan-age-uke* (Rising Block vs. Attack to the Head)

*Jodan-age-uke* is used mainly to block punching attacks coming in above the height of the solar plexus.

### Technique
*(Figs 112–116)*
The block is often practised by first placing the left arm above the head, with the hand open but in the *age-uke* position, and then lowering it as you simultaneously raise the right arm. The right elbow is kept close to the side as the forearm moves out forwards, slightly away from the body, creating enough space for the left arm to be lowered behind it. The two arms form a cross in front of the face with the right, blocking arm being in front of the arm being lowered as they pass one another. The left arm is pulled down and back onto the side just above the hip as the right arm is snapped into position, the forearm and wrist rotating so that the inside edge of the forearm is uppermost, just above the top of the forehead.

The blocking area is a 10cm (4in) section running from the bony part of the wrist almost to mid-forearm. The rotation of the forearm coupled with that of the hips, and drive from the rear leg are especially important. The forearm and wrist action add power to the block and increase the effect of deflection, guiding the incoming attack away from its target. The initial contact of the block with the incoming arm should ideally, if the timing of the block is correct, be relatively far away from the head, perhaps 30 to 45 cm (12 to 18in) with a very tall defender, which gives more time for deflecting it up and over. Sometimes, these ideal conditions cannot be met and the block has to be made in a last, split second, using speed and impact to knock the blow away and achieve the deflection, rather than catching and redirecting it.

The block is usually practised with the defender in the ready position. The attacker steps in with a *jodan-oi-zuki* (lunge punch to the face). Here, the defender anticipates the attack and steps forwards into *zenkutsu-dachi* to make the block. Once the block has been performed the defender can instantly counter attack, in this case with *chudan-gyaku-zuki* (reverse punch to the midsection). Notice how the blocking position with the correct stance and right hand held ready on the hip allows the defender to generate maximum power by pulling down the blocking hand and turning the hips as he punches. Aim to block with your elbow at about the height of your ear, and as close to it as possible. If it is too far away it will be difficult to generate sufficient tension in the muscles of the side. Note also the turning action of the forearm in Figs 114 and 115.

*Fig 112   Detail of correct placement and angulation of the wrist and forearm in jodan-age-uke.*

*Fig 113*

*Fig 114*

*Fig 115*

*Fig 116*

### *Chudan-uchi-uke* (Inner Block Against Midsection Attack)

This block is used against attacks aimed at the solar plexus, chest and midsection.

### Technique
*(Figs 117–120 )*

With the defender in ready stance, the attacker steps forward to attack with *chudan-oi-zuki* (lunge punch to the midsection). The defender steps back on to his right leg, crossing his arms as he does so by placing the right arm out in front of him and crossing the left across his chest, protecting the solar plexus. As he adopts *zenkutsu-dachi* his left arm describes an arc, coming under his right arm, up and across his midsection as the left arm is pulled back to the punching ready position. The blocking action of the arm is accompanied by the turning of the hips, the thumb side of the wrist and forearm contacting with the thumb side of the attacker's punching arm, deflecting it outside the line of the defender's body. At the moment of contact the elbow should be bent at 90 degrees and the muscles of the back and arm tensed. The elbow must be kept close to the body. If it drifts too far away it will lack power, as it will not be possible to tense the muscles of the back and armpit effectively. This block leaves the attacker wide open to a counter-attack such as *gyaku-zuki*, but here *nihon-nukite* (two finger spear hand) is demonstrated. Once again, the hip rotation of the blocking action not only adds power to the block, but it also creates a position from which the defender can generate considerable power with his counter attack.

*Fig 117*

*Fig 118*

*Fig 119*

*Fig 120*

## *Chudan-soto-uke* (Outer Block Against Midsection Attack)

The outer block is used like the inner block to deal with attacks aimed at the midsection, and is the only block in this group in which the arms are not crossed.

### Technique
*(Figs 121–124)*
As the attacker steps in with a punching attack, the defender steps back on to his right foot, raising his right arm out in front of him. At the same time he lifts his left arm up, raising the elbow and just touching his left ear with the knuckles of his left fist. As the defender steps into his defensive stance, he forcefully pulls the right hand back to his hip as he turns his hips and strikes his opponent's punching arm, bringing down the bony inside edge of his left wrist and forearm, and twisting the fist and forearm as the block connects, to increase the amount of deflection. The blocking arm rotates through 180 degrees, the back of the fist turning so that it faces the opponent at the level of his chin.

As the block is completed, the defender is perfectly placed to counter-attack and, twisting the hips forcefully as he pulls back the blocking hand, counters to his opponent's exposed body with *gyaku-zuki*.

*Fig 122*

*Fig 123*

*Fig 121*

*Fig 124*

## *Gedan-barai* (Downward Block)

*Gedan-barai* is used against attacks aimed at waist level and below. The basic *gedan barai* is the standard block against kicking attacks aimed from knee to waist height and is also used against punches aimed at the stomach or lower abdomen.

### *Gedan barai* vs *Mae-geri*
### (Figs 125–128 )

Attacker and defender face each other, both in left free-fighting *kamae*. The attacker attempts *mae-geri*, lifting his rear foot off the ground and bringing his knee up high into the correct kicking position. As soon as the rear foot moves, the defender reacts, dropping his right arm out in front of him and bending his left arm, so that his left fist almost touches the right side of his jaw. This intermediate position is important because it protects the defender's chest and solar plexus area and allows him to switch to protect his head should the attacker change his plans suddenly. It also puts him in a position where he can get full power into the block that is to follow. The block is delivered as the leg extends, by striking downwards with the bent left arm, deflecting the foot by contacting with the outside edge of the wrist and forearm against the inside of the leg. If the target is your groin, the block will have to be lower than the one shown in the photographs which show a kick to the solar plexus.

The blocking arm is strongest about 15cm(6in) above the front knee. Bending the front knee and getting the hips low is vital, as is ensuring adequate hip turn. If the block lacks power and snap against a powerful technique like a front kick to the groin, or a roundhouse kick, the kick will crash through the block rather than be deflected. This technique should be practised to the left and to the right, and stepping forwards into the block and stepping backwards, retreating from the kick, so that all eventualities are covered.

When blocking powerful kicks, you must have confidence in your blocking technique. If you allow your opponent's speed and power to intimidate you, then when you block you may hesitate or try to keep the hips back out of range, making your blocking action weaker and therefore ineffective. You must train the block until you have real belief in it. Remember to get your hips low, and get as close as possible to the opponent when you make the block.

Against fast kickers and punchers you should, at all times, keep out of range. This means that if they want to hit you they must take a step to get in striking distance. That step is the telegraph which gives you time to come up with an adequate defence or counter. If you allow a faster fighter to stand close enough to hit you without his having to take a step, you make his task that much easier. Remember to maintain correct fighting distance for your relative speeds and limb lengths.

*Fig 125*

*Fig 126*

*Fig 127*

*Fig 128    Blocks may not always look spectacular, but they are necessary. An effective gedan-barai can prevent all kinds of painful blows from reaching the target and could have stopped this front kick from crashing into the defender's abdomen.*

## *Gedan-barai* (Block as Counter)

*(Figs 129–135 )*

The crossing action of the arms in blocking is extremely important, and *gedan-barai* is no exception. This sequence illustrates how the preparatory movements of the block can actually become blocks in their own right, allowing the major blocking action to become a countering strike in its own right.

This kind of block crashing into an opponent can be extremely disconcerting and may preclude the need for a follow-up strike, which says something about the mechanical efficiency of karate techniques.

*Fig 129    Forearm rotation and action of the blocking arm in gedan-barai.*

*Fig 130    The attacker is in left zenkutsu-dachi and the defender is in ready stance, anticipating a punching attack to the midsection.*

*Fig 131    The initial attack is a feint aimed at the stomach, but the attacker punches to the face instead. The defender simply uses the left hand which is placed in position ready to block the body punch, to do gedan-barai to block the punch to the face.*

*Fig 132    Then he immediately slams his gedan-barai into the attacker's solar plexus, contacting with the fist, rather than with the wrist and forearm.*

*Fig 133    The attacker's punch has almost reached the defender before he has time to bring his arm down in an effective gedan-barai. The leading right arm deflects the attack, the thumb edge of the wrist contacting with the attacker's wrist.*

*Fig 134    The actual gedan-barai then crashes down into the attacker's solar plexus, and the defender is in a perfect position...*

*Fig 135    ... to follow up with a reverse punch.*

## *Shuto-uke* (Knife Hand Block and Counter)

*(Figs 136–139 )*

The knife hand blocks are fundamental and among the most effective in karate. In free sparring, it can be dangerous to use them, as an open hand is more easily hurt or injured by a kick than the closed fist would be. Knife hands serve a double function, as both blocking and striking techniques. When the knife hand is delivered against an extended fist or foot, it should strike as if to cut off the opponent's limb with a sword. There are many variations.

*Fig 136    Both fighters are in left free fighting stance.*

*Fig 137    The attacker comes in with a powerful lunge punch. The defender steps in to him on his right leg, lifting his right hand so that the thumb is level with his left ear, deflecting the incoming punch.*

*Fig 138    The left arm is extended in front of the body and covers the midsection, the right thumb is held by the right ear. The blocking action is performed in kokutsu-dachi.*

*Fig 139    The reverse knife hand is used to strike the side of the attacker's neck. As the right arm slashes into the attacker's neck, the hips twist and the left hand is pulled back on to the left hip. The knife hand here is demonstrated as a strike, but it is often used as a pure blocking technique, just like gedan-barai in the previous example.*

## *Morote-uke* (Two Handed or Augmented Blocks)

These techniques are advised for use against more powerful adversaries, whose techniques may be too powerful to block using normal methods. The inner block (*uchi-uke*) can be reinforced by bracing the forearm with the other fist. There is a considerable variety of such techniques, but space does not permit a detailed description of them here. They include: *morote-sukui-uke* (two handed scooping block)used for applying pressure to the knee when blocking kicks; *kakiwake-uke* (reverse wedge block), used for breaking two-handed grips on the lapels, *morote-tsukami-uke* (two-handed grasping block), which involves blocking and grabbing an opponent's punching arm to throw him off balance.These blocks are all advanced techniques that are not often seen or used very much. The most commonly used two-handed block is *juji-uke*, the X-block.

*Fig 140*

## *Juji-uke* (X-Block)
*(Figs 140–143 )*

The X-block is normally used against kicks to the groin and punches to the face. It is very strong, but requires the karateka's full commitment, and inevitably leaves other areas unprotected when it is performed. It is important to understand that it is best used as as a trapping block and normally should be followed up immediately with a locking or throwing technique.

*Fig 141*

In this sequence, the attacker uses *mae-geri* and the defender protects himself by lifting both arms and crossing his hands at shoulder height. As the kick flicks out, he drives both arms down, the wrists forming a cross which is the point of contact with attacker's shin, ankle or instep. Having blocked the technique, he grabs the leg as shown and twists the knee, forcing the attacker off balance to such an extent that he falls to the floor. He would then be immediately pinned with a leg lock or finished off with a punching or stamping technique.

*Fig 142*

*Fig 143*

87

Fig 144 *Shotokan stylist George Best scores spectacularly with an ushiro-mawashi-geri in an international match for Great Britain vs. France.*

# 4 Leg Techniques

*'Use what works, discard what doesn't.'*
Bill Wallace

## LEGS

Legs are stronger than arms and they are also longer, which makes kicking techniques among the most effective and most powerful natural weapons that the body possesses. Not only does a good kick give the kicker a reach advantage over an adversary relying on punching or grabbing, but it allows the full power of the legs to be directly channelled into a strike. Legs are approximately four times stronger than arms, so the force generated by an expert can be considerable. Legs can be used for blocking, hooking and sweeping an opponent, as well as for kicking.

## DYNAMICS OF EFFECTIVE KICKING

The weight of the whole body should be behind a good kick, and this is best achieved by thrusting forwards with the hips. Ankles, knees and hips should all be flexed as the leg muscles drive the foot into the target, to absorb the counter shock of impact. Kicking techniques, while more spectacular and potentially more powerful than techniques done with the hands, are more difficult to learn and require constant repetition and practice. We use our hands for countless tasks in everyday life, and the hands co-ordinate with eye and brain a lot faster and more easily than do the feet. As weapons, though, the feet are less prone to damage, and in most self defence situations, shoes are worn, further reducing the possibility of harm to the foot from kicking.

## WARM-UP AND FLEXIBILITY

An important factor in good kicking is the combination of relaxation and flexibility which permits fast, accurate kicking. It is vitally important that the muscles of the legs, groin, hips and lower back are all thoroughly warmed up and stretched before a session of serious kick training. Not warming up beforehand is an invitation to injury: some of the muscles involved in many of the kicking actions are thin strands or sheets of muscle that are easily damaged by sudden unprepared over-exertion. A pulled muscle can be quite serious, possibly taking a considerable time to heal, and can set back your progress, so avoidance is better than cure. Always stretch and warm up the lower body thoroughly. The importance of this cannot be over-stressed.

## BALANCE

An important consideration in all kicking techniques is that of balance. If you are not on balance when you kick, you can easily fall or be knocked over. One of the major points in most karate systems is that, when kicking, the foot of the supporting leg should be flat on the floor. If the heel of the supporting foot is raised, stability is reduced. It is more difficult to deliver a kick while moving than it is when stationary, and it is certainly harder to connect with a moving target than with a stationary one. The supporting leg in most kicks should bend at the knee, though not too much, or the techniques will slow down and lack snap, and it should be flexed at the ankle.

## PULL-BACK

Many karateka train in techniques to counter kicks, which involve catching the leg and throwing the opponent. This can be devastatingly effective when done well, and is usually followed up with a finishing-off technique on the ground, such as a punching or stamping technique. In order to avoid falling victim to such a counter, it is vital to practise pulling back the leg as quickly as you push it out, after you do the kick.

Some fighters in competition like to leave the foot on the target, to give the referees time to see the score, for instance when they do a roundhouse kick to the head. A good referee should need no such help, and doing so invites a throw or sweeping counter.

## KICKING FOR COMPETITION AND SELF DEFENCE

It is worth distinguishing between the kind of techniques that are practical and advisable from a self defence viewpoint, and those primarily intended for training or competition situations. Standing kicks to the head, while good as exercises for developing and demonstrating flexibility, would probably be inappropriate in a self defence situation. An expert is probably capable of incapacitating an attacker with whatever technique he chooses, but a short, sharp strike to the jaw is so much easier and safer than a high kick. Generally, karate teachers advise their students not to aim to kick above waist or chest height, the knee and the groin are preferred targets.

Other techniques that would rarely be used in a self defence context include the jumping front and side kicks. These kicks were originally devised for unhorsing mounted opponents. They are rarely used in contest because it is impossible to change direction in mid-flight, and all an opponent has to do is step to one side to avoid being hit and to position himself perfectly to counter the kick. Some karateka argue that these kicks have

*Fig 145   High kicks may be spectacular and effective in competition, but they are not recommended for self defence.*

surprise value. That is indisputable if you are facing an unskilled adversary, but a very different matter if up against someone who is an experienced brawler or streetfighter.

Women, while generally a lot weaker in terms of upper body muscular development and strength do not lag so far behind in terms of leg strength, and are usually capable of acquiring good flexibility rapidly, since they tend not to have so much muscular bulk. Kicking practice is therefore extremely beneficial for them, because it allows them to train one of their strong points.

In both self defence and contest situations, the energy of the kick has to be focused into the smallest possible area. Different techniques use different striking areas; the front kick and roundhouse use the ball of the foot or instep, the back kick and reverse roundhouse the heel, the side kick the outer edge of the foot, and so on.

It is important to practise kicking on the move, as follow-ups to punches and immediately after blocking so that they become spontaneously easy, natural responses to given combative situations. The best fighters can usually kick almost equally well with either leg and, curiously, in many experiments the non-preferred leg is often found to be fractionally faster than the preferred leg, if not necessarily more accurate or more powerful, which are also important considerations.

True ambidexterity, the ability to use both the left and right sides equally well, is rare, but it is the ideal to aim for as it makes the karateka doubly effective. Being able to kick well with both legs means that kicks can come from any angle and in all sorts of difficult-to-defend against flurries with varied feints and combinations.

## THE FEET AS WEAPONS

Just as the various parts of the hand can be used as weapons, so too can the different parts of the feet. Different kicks involve using different parts of the foot to focus the energy of the technique.

## Koshi (Ball of Foot)
*(Fig 146)*
The ball of the foot is used for kicks such as *mae-geri* (front kick) and *mawashi-geri* (roundhouse kick). The toes are curled upwards allowing contact to be made with the ball of the foot to virtually any part of the opponent's body or head. Normal targets include the groin, stomach, solar plexus, throat, jaw and sides. To increase effectiveness, the instep should be tensed on impact and the ankle of the kicking foot flexed.

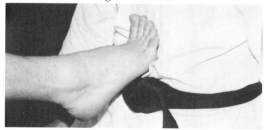

*Fig 146    Koshi, the ball of the foot.*

## Sokuto (Outside Edge of Foot)
*(Fig 147)*
The use of the outside edge of the foot is typical in *yoko-geri* (side kick). It is better than stamping with the sole of the foot as it focuses the power into a smaller area. In modern karate the big toe is usually curled upwards, but it used to be popular to turn it downwards. The main difference is that the former method allows greater ankle flexibility, but the old method is generally felt to allow the kicker to tighten the muscles of the foot more easily. *Sokuto* is particularly useful in self defence for stamping kicks to the side or back of the knee, like *fumikomi*.

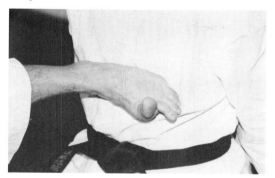

*Fig 147    Sokuto, the outside edge of the foot.*

## Haisoku (Instep)
*(Fig 148–149)*
The instep can be used instead of the ball of the foot for *mawashi-geri* and to make a very fast snap kick attack to the groin (*kin-geri*). The foot should be stretched so that the toes point downwards.

*Fig 148    Haisoku, the instep, used here to attack the groin with kin-geri.*

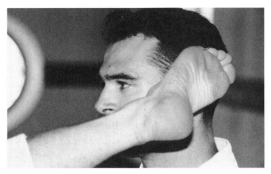

Fig 149   *Haisoku used instead of koshi to do mawashi-geri.*

Fig 150   *The heel can be used for doing axe kicks...*

## Kakato (Heel)

*(Fig 150–151)*

The heel can be used in a variety of stamping kicks, and is especially effective with *ushiro-geri* or *yoko-geri*. Some styles do an axe kick, where the leg is swung high above the opponent's head and brought crashing down on either his head or collar-bone. The point of contact for this technique is usually the heel.

## Tsumasaki (Tips of toes)

*(Fig 152)*

*Tsumasaki* is the foot equivalent of a *nukite*. The toes are driven straight into the target, usually a soft part of the body, such as the groin area or midsection. On Okinawa this type of kick was regarded as being particularly effective, as it increased the kicker's range and penetration for groin attacks.

Fig 151 *...and for ushiro-geri, back kick.*

Fig 152   *Tsumasaki, the straight-toed kick to the groin.*

Fig 153   *Abdu Shaher, World Lightweight Champion, attacking with mawashi-geri, using the instep.*

### *Mae-geri-kekomi* (Front Thrust Kick)
*(Fig 154–156)*

There are two basic types of *mae-geri* or front kick: the snap kick (*keage*) and the thrust kick (*kekomi*). The former is quicker and can be done off the front leg to surprise an opponent. The thrust kick, however, is much more powerful. *Mae-geri-kekomi* is the easiest kick for beginners to learn, particularly those who have have good muscle tone in the legs and a certain amount of foot and eye co-ordination from having previously played sports such as football and rugby.

In karate competition the striking point is the ball of the foot. The instep may be used if the groin is a target, or if the adversary is doubled over. Groin kicks, however, are not normally allowed in training or competition. The most difficult aspects of the kick for most beginners are *ma-ai*, or the distance between the kicker and the target, and the timing. Covering the necessary distance to land the kick is also a problem when the karateka has not yet developed the speed and agility to cover distance quickly. Many also forget to pull the foot back after kicking, which may mean the leg gets caught and they get swept.

*Fig 154    The attacker is in left stance, his partner in right.*

*Fig 155    The attacker transfers his weight from his back leg on to his left foot, using the thrust developed by the rear leg to pick the knee up high, between 45 to 60 degrees...*

*Fig 156    ...and kicks, using the power of the legs and hips, targeting the midsection and striking with the ball of the foot.*

### *Mae-geri-keage* (Front Snap Kick)
*(Fig 157–160)*

The snap kick, which is usually performed off the front leg, is quicker to perform than the front thrust kick. The distance from the front foot to the opponent is shorter, and so too is the distance the foot moves, since it does not come from behind. The price of this is a considerable reduction in power, but the technique does have surprise value and can be used as a stepping action to close with the opponent.

The leading leg is quickly picked up and the foot snapped out at the target. It is instantly pulled back and returned to the ground or, if the opponent moves back from the kick, a step can be taken to follow him. The kicking leg remains the leading leg. The reach and speed of the technique can be increased by making a skipping or jumping step with the back foot in order to get closer to the opponent, and by way of anticipating his evasive reaction prior to actually kicking.

Another variation on the front kick is to step through with the rear leg, which is the left if you are in right *zenkutsu-dachi*, as if intending to do a basic thrust kick. This is just a feint; instead of kicking, you make a jumping step, putting the left leg down in front of you, and drive through with the right. This feint serves a double function – drawing the opponent's block and increasing the distance the kicker can cover in the attack.

*Fig 157*

*Fig 158*

*Fig 159*

*Fig 160*

*Fig 161   The importance of immediately pulling back the leg after kicking cannot be over-emphasized, whether in self defence or contest. A well-trained opponent will often try to catch the kicking leg then sweep away the supporting leg, as in this example from the 1988 WUKO European Championships in Genoa, to throw the kicker to the ground and follow up with a punch. Generally, the higher the kick, the easier it is to counter.*

## *Yoko-geri* (Side Kick)

### (Figs 162–164)

The *yoko-geri*, or side kick, requires good flexibility in the hips and was originally conceived as a weapon that could be used against adversaries attacking from the right and left in a 'back to the wall' situation where the karateka defending himself assumes *kiba-dachi* or horse stance and waits for his attackers to come to him. There are also a side thrust kick and a side snap kick, which have different applications.

The side kick has grown in popularity in competition karate as a result of fighters taking up a side-on stance, to present a smaller target area to their opponents' direct punching and kicking attacks. Good exponents can use the *keage* version of this kick much as boxers use the jab, to stun and jolt an opponent without getting hit themselves. Semi-contact fighters can glide or hop in and poke out the side kick to score points. Full contact fighters need to generate more power, and this is achieved by stepping in and driving out the kick. The side thrust kick off the back leg is a more powerful technique than the side snap kick off the forward leg, but the snap kick is quicker as it does not have as far to travel.

*Fig 162   Both fighters are in left free-fighting stance.*

*Fig 163 The kicker pivots on the ball of the left foot, turning the hips through 180 degrees so that his right side faces his opponent. He lifts the right knee high flexing the ankle as he does so...*

*Fig 164   ...and thrusts out his right leg, striking the side of his opponent's neck with the outer edge of the foot.*

### Key Points in Yoko-geri-kekomi

• Fast hip rotation and high knee lift are crucial to the effectiveness of this kick.
• Flexibility in the hips and legs is very important because the hip muscles generate the real power in this kick. Any tightness or lack of mobility will slow the kick down and reduce its effectiveness.
• After kicking, the kicker should recover his original position without losing his balance. This helps to develop control in the co-ordination of the stomach, leg and hip muscles, necessary to do good side kicks.
• This recovery practice also teaches the kicker not to leave the leg sticking out.

*Fig 165    Middleweight World Champion Jose Egea of Spain scores ippon with a superbly focused yoko-geri-kekomi to the ribs/side chest of an opponent. Note the supporting foot flat on the floor, providing stability, and the way Egea's hips have opened as he kicks.*

*Fig 166    British international Mervyn Etienne uses his long legs to good advantage to attack fellow British team member Mike Sailsman with yoko-geri.*

## *Mawashi-geri* (Roundhouse Kick)
### *(Figs 167–171)*

The archetypal karate kick, the *mawashi-geri*, or roundhouse kick, is useful against adversaries who take up a sideways-on stance, since it allows the karateka to kick around the guard into the front or back of the body. It can also be used successfully to the opponent's sides or ribs, and even to the head if the karateka is very flexible. A well-focused well-controlled *mawashi-geri* to the head almost always earns ippon in semi-contact, but is a much more difficult technique to land in full contact, where fighters are more highly trained in the skills of ducking, bobbing and weaving to avoid punches and kicks.

The roundhouse kick can be done off the front or rear leg. In Shotokan the ball of the foot is usually used as the striking area, whereas in Wado-Ryu the instep is preferred. The Shotokan technique, which involves turning the hip out to the side and making a big rotational movement of the hips is more powerful, but also more obvious and a little slower than the Wado-Ryu method.

In the Wado-style kick, the knee is lifted in front of the body, just as for *mae-geri*, and then the hips turn, making it a much more difficult technique for the opponent to read. Many Wado stylists who have reached the pinnacle of semi-contact sport karate, such as Eugene Codrington, Geoff Thompson and Vic Charles, were able to use this technique to very good effect at the highest level of WUKO competition, so it is worthy of study whatever style you actually prefer to practise. In semi-contact competition, top competitors prefer to hit with the instep to reduce the risk of injury to the opponent. British international karate competitor and World champion Geoff Thompson once ruptured a Sri Lankan opponent's spleen with *mawashi-geri*, which gives some idea of how powerful it can be.

*Fig 167  The basic mawashi-geri off the rear leg. Both fighters are in left stance.*

*Fig 168  The kicker lifts his knee high and out to the side of his body, then rotates his hips, spinning...*

## TOBI-GERI (JUMPING KICKS)
### *(Fig 172)*

A group of kicks not so far considered are the jumping kicks, such as *tobi-mae-geri* (jumping front kick), *tobi-yoko-geri* (jumping side kick), *nidan-geri* (double kick) and *kesa-geri* (diagonal kick). The jumping kicks are generally part of the karate heritage and many were invented for use against mounted enemies, often in hilly terrain, where it would be possible to attack from above. They are of dubious value against an unmounted opponent because it is not possible to change direction once an attack is launched, and it is a relatively easy matter to side-step such attacks. They do, however, have considerable value as a form of pylometric training. Jumping develops great spring and explosive strength in the legs, making the karateka stronger, fitter and more agile, so

*Fig 169    ...on the ball of the foot of his supporting leg, kicks his opponent in the head, using the instep.*

*Fig 170    He then pulls back his foot and hip and...*

*Fig 171    ...returns to his original stance.*

they certainly have a place in modern as well as in traditional training programmes. Many people enjoy doing them too as it allows them to make a maximum effort, as they imagine trying to dislodge a mounted attacker. It is especially useful to do these kicks striking against a kick shield or focus pad.

*Fig 172    Flying side kick against a kick shield.*

*Fig 173    Shotokan star Frank Brennan scores ippon with left jodan-mawashi-geri.*

*Fig 174    The top fighters are usually ambidextrous. Compare with Fig 173 above. Frank Brennan scores with a right chudan-mawashi-geri. Photograph by Tim Green.*

*Fig 175   A Kyokushinkai stylist displays excellent poise and stability in semi-contact competition.*

*Fig 176   Shotokan expert Elwyn Hall unleashing a superbly accurate chudan-ushiro-geri in semi-contact competition.*

## *Ushiro-mawashi-geri* (Back Roundhouse Kick)
### (Figs 177–179)

*Ushiro-mawashi* evolved out of the turning movement used to deliver *ushiro-geri*, but instead of thrusting the leg straight out it is swung and lifted in an arc, the heel being used to strike the target. The main difference in the build up is that the knee is not raised during the turn, the foot rather describing a large semi-circular arc from the floor to the target, usually the head. The power is generated by the twisting of the hips and the straightening of the legs.

*Fig 177*

## *Ushiro-geri* (Back Kick)
### (Figs 177, 180–181)

*Ushiro-geri* was probably originally conceived as a technique for dealing with an adversary who attempted to attack from behind in a situation involving more than one attacker. Sometimes referred to as a mule or horse kick in some styles, it is a very powerful technique, though risky in competition because it is necessary to turn the back to the opponent, offering a tempting and easy-to-hit target if the technique is not done very quickly or if it misses.

The starting position is the same as for *ushiro-mawashi-geri* (Fig 177). The kick can be done by stepping and spinning on the ball of the front foot, or by spinning without stepping. The kicker spins on his front foot, turning through 180 degrees, quickly spinning the head and looking over the right shoulder (the same side of the body as the leg he is going to kick with), as he lifts his knee to waist height. Using the momentum generated by the spin he thrusts from his hip, driving the leg straight into his opponent's midsection.

*Fig 180*

*Ushiro-geri* is often favoured by heavier, stronger karateka as it is a technique which it is easy to get your bodyweight into. It is most effective, however, when performed by faster fighters. It is usually used to attack to the mid section, and can be combined with spinning backfist or *ushiro-mawashi-geri* or *yoko-geri*, to pose a quadruple threat.

*Fig 181*

*Fig 178*

*Fig 179*

*Fig 182   George Best, one of Britain's top Shotokan exponents, attacks with a fine example of ushiro-mawashi-geri.*

### *Fumikomi* (Stamping Kick)
*(Fig 183–184)*

Like *fumikiri*, *fumikomi* is a self defence technique. It is a stamping kick, generally delivered slightly to the side or rear, which can attack the shin or instep and which is particularly effective against the knee joint. It can also be used to attack the supporting leg of anyone attempting a kicking attack, with knee injury being an extremely likely result.

### *Fumikiri* (Cutting Kick)
*(Fig 185)*

*Fumikiri* is delivered like a thrust kick and is normally used to attack the shin or instep in self defence applications. If shoes are worn, the technique usually barks and scrapes the shin.

### *Hiza-geri* (Knee Strike)
*(Figs 186–187)*

*Hiza-geri* is not normally seen in semi-contact or full contact matches, but is used in Kyokushinkai knockdown competitions. It is a very powerful technique for self defence purposes. It can be used at very close range, most effectively to knee an attacker in the groin, or by grabbing an adversary around the back of the neck, then bending him over and kneeing him in the thorax or face. Grabbing by the hair and kneeing the luckless victim in the face is a favourite tactic of muggers and experienced streetfighters. A well-placed knee in the face will usually result in black eyes and a broken nose.

*Fig 184*

*Fig 185*

*Fig 186*

*Fig 183*

*Fig 187*

## *Ashi-gake*
### (Figs 188–193)

Gake means 'to hook or uproot' and is a foot technique which, rather than sweeping an opponent off his feet, hooks his leg to uproot him, breaking his balance. Often when attacked with *ashi-gake* an opponent does not fall down, but just as usefully he can be spun or turned into an extremely disadvantageous position. Usually, *ashi-gake* is used to turn the opponent from a sideways stance, so that you can get behind him and punch or kick at his exposed back. At other times, the hook is inwards, splitting his stance and loss of balance may even be serious enough to force him to drop his hands on to the ground in an all-fours position, leaving him wide open to a variety of techniques. This technique can be especially useful to long-legged men.

*Fig 188*

*Fig 191*

*Fig 189*

*Fig 192*

*Fig 190*

*Fig 193*

## LEG BLOCKS (JAMMING)

As well as being used for kicking, the legs can be used to block kicking attacks. The advantage of using the legs rather than the arms is that the hands remain free to deal with any subsequent punching attacks, or for counter-attacking. It is also frequently less painful to block powerful kicking attacks with the legs than with the fore-arms. Jamming an opponent's kicks, which can be very painful on the kicker's shins and leg muscles, can also discourage him from trying them.

*Fig 194*

## BLOCKING A SIDE KICK WITH THE SHIN (HOOKING BLOCK)

*(Figs 194–196)*

In a free-fighting situation as the opponent lifts his leg and tries to side kick you, immediately lift your own front leg and block by hooking his ankle with your shin. Keep your knee high and close to your body after blocking, so as to be able to move or counter appropriately.

*Fig 195*

*Fig 196*

## JAMMING THE FRONT KICK (PRESSING BLOCK)

*(Fig 197)*

This technique requires good anticipation. As the attacker goes to lift his kicking leg immediately step in and stamp the sole of your foot into his shin. The harder he tries to kick, the more painful the result will be for him. It is possible to do this with either foot.

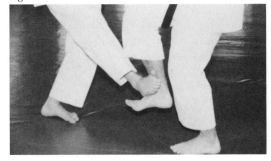

*Fig 197*

*Fig 198   An augmented block, using the knee and both hands to nullify a powerful mawashi-geri attack. Smothering a technique in this way is theoretically less effective and less desirable as a strategy than a crisp block and counter or even a quick evasion, but against strong, agile opponents, sometimes there is little alternative. This type of technique is more typical of full contact bouts, where avoiding being hurt is more of a concern than looking good.*

## *ASHI-WAZA* (FOOT-SWEEPS)

Foot-sweeps are throwing techniques used to sweep or trip an opponent. The aim of the foot-sweep is always to get the opponent off balance, so that you can hit him more easily with a punch or a kick. In other sports, like judo, a point may be awarded for cleanly throwing the opponent on to his back. In karate competition, an effective sweep, while just as dramatic and impressive, does not score a point on its own. It must be followed up with a punch or kick. Throwing the opponent with a foot-sweep is even more difficult in karate than in judo as the karateka has to close distance and optionally grab and sweep simultaneously.

Foot-sweeps are excellent for confusing and distracting opponents and setting them up for other techniques. In self defence they are very useful, and may be sufficient on their own to discourage a would-be assailant. Foot-sweeps are usually more effective when assisted by a grab and tug from a free hand, but it is virtually impossible to do this in top level competition without being scored upon with a kick or punch. Even when the opponent goes down cleanly, the danger of being countered with a kick as you move in to finish him off is real and ever present.

## Technique

There are four components to an effective foot-sweep: distance, timing, balance and breathing. Distance is determined through practice and depends upon the relative height, leg length and speed of the two opponents. Timing must be learned, and will vary according to the stances adopted; it is the essence of good sweeping techniques and is closely linked to breathing: attack just as your opponent is about to breathe in, or just after he exhales and is about to take his next breath. Balance is determined by stance and reaction time, and you must be able to identify in which direction your opponent can be swept most easily.

Apart from direct attacks, footsweeps also function extremely effectively as counter techniques, especially when your opponent tries to kick. With only one foot on the floor, his balance is already compromised. There is a variety of useful takedowns that are performed after first catching the kicking leg and then sweeping the supporting leg.

### *Ashi-barai* (Foot-sweep)
*(Figs 199–201)*

*Ashi-barai* is the basic foot-sweep. Step forward and sweep your opponent's forward leg in the direction that his toes are pointing. Perfect timing and contact involves striking with the sole of your foot against the outside edge of his foot or heel, as he steps on to the foot you attack. In this case he will drop as if he had stepped on a patch of ice or a banana skin. Many karateka do not devote enough time to finding the right timing and technique for foot sweeps, tending just to crash a kick into their opponent's lower leg, somewhere on the side of the shin or calf, between the ankle and the knee. This can work if the opponent has a weak stance, but really is a crude and ineffective way to sweep someone. In *zenkutsu-dachi* the opponent's weak point is his front leg. However, if he is in a solid stance, it cannot be simply swept away in a direct sideways movement. It is much better to place your foot behind his heel and sweep his foot in a forward direction, causing his stance to lengthen and making him fall. Better still, do it as he is stepping and just about to put his weight on the front foot.

### *Ashi-barai-nidan* (Double Foot-sweep)
*(Figs 202–204)*

If your partner defends by changing his stance and adopts *kokutsu-dachi*, with his weight supported principally on his bent rear leg, you might attack his front foot just as a feint to get him to lift it and put all his weight on to his rear leg, then double up your sweep, taking his rear leg. When the feet are close together in this way it is an easy matter to throw him to his rear.

**Tip**

In *zenkutsu-dachi* the opponent's weak point is his front leg. However, if he is in a solid stance, it cannot be simply swept away in a direct sideways movement. It is better to place your foot behind his heel and sweep his foot in a forward direction, causing his stance to lengthen and making him fall. Better still, do it as he is stepping and just about to put his weight on the front foot.

Fig 202

Fig 199

Fig 203

Fig 200

Fig 201

Fig 204

## Foot-sweep Counter to *Yoko-geri*
*(Figs 205–209)*

There are a number of possibilities when confronting any kicking attack. One is to try to catch the kicking leg and sweep away the supporting leg in order to throw your adversary to the ground. This sort of technique should, for obvious reasons, only be practised on mats. Both partners should also have received instruction in safe falling technique before trying these techniques. The most important thing is to co-operate, and help support your partner, lowering him rather than crashing him to the floor. The person being swept should concentrate on keeping the chin tucked in to the chest and exhaling sharply as he lands. If you hold your breath you can be winded, just as you would be by being kicked in the stomach.

The attacker comes in with *yoko-geri*. The defender side-steps and does a scooping block, catching the outstretched leg. He steps in to his opponent and lifts the leg as high as possible in a single, quick movement. The aim is to push the kicker off balance over his standing leg, perhaps even to get him hopping. If his supporting foot can be made to leave the ground he can then be swept effortlessly. At the very least, try to get him up on to his toes. Sweep the supporting foot away with a scything action of your foot. Be sure to grab his gi, and control his fall with the hand that is not holding the leg. As he lands flat on his back, follow up immediately with a stamping kick or punch. This technique is equally feasible against a *mae-geri* attack.

*Fig 206*

*Fig 207*

*Fig 208*

*Fig 205*

*Fig 209*

## Foot-sweep Counter to *Mawashi-geri*
*(Figs 210–213)*

This is similar to the previous technique, but where the first throw was directly to the rear, this technique utilizes a circular turning motion, to make blocking and throwing the roundhouse kick easier. The attacker throws a roundhouse kick to your head. Step inside, gathering his leg up with a scooping action of your arm at the same time. Quickly grab his lapel or, in a self defence situation, place the palm of your hand against his face or, for a really heavy fall, under his chin. (*N.B.* The hand should only be placed under the chin for self defence purposes, as the kicker will land on the back of his head and probably be concussed by the fall.) Immediately make a half-step turn and sweep away his supporting leg, throwing him to the floor. The effectiveness of the sweep in this throw will be increased by pointing the toes. As his back hits the floor, immediately follow up with a punch to the groin, solar plexus or other vulnerable area.

*Fig 212*

*Fig 210*

*Fig 211*

*Fig 213*

## DEVELOPING KICKING SKILLS
*(Figs 214–224)*

Top full contact fighters like 'Superfoot' Bill Wallace have shown how it is possible to combine the leg action from the knee with *mae-geri*, *ma-washi-geri* and *yoko-geri* in spectacular combinations. *Renzoku-geri*, or combination kicking, is very spectacular and very good for building stamina and explosive gymnastic power, as the legs have to work very hard. There are numerous other kicks and feints that are best studied after reaching black belt, these include: *Mikazuki-geri* (crescent kick), *ushiro-mikazuki-geri* (reverse crescent kick) and *gyaku-mawashi-geri* (reverse roundhouse kick).

*Fig 214   Kicks can be used very effectively as stopping techniques. Here the attacker is about to attack with a lunge punch. The defender anticipates his intentions and pivots on his front foot, turning to his left...*

*Fig 217   In this technique the attacker is in a left stance and the defender is in a right stance.*

*Fig 218   The attacker tries a stepping punch, but the defender pivots on his right foot and moves his body to avoid the attack by bringing his right foot behind him in a quarter circle.*

*Fig 221   ...and delivering a yoko-geri (side-kick) to his midsection. This can be followed up...*

*Fig 222   ...with a side kick to the jaw.*

*Fig 215    ... lifting his right knee high, he spins on the ball of his left foot, he turns his head to look at his target...*

*Fig 216    ...and he snaps out an ushiro-geri (back kick) into his opponent's mid-section, checking his attack.*

*Fig 219    This step puts him in a position where he can easily snap an ura-mawashi-geri (back roundhouse, or hook kick) into his opponent's face.*

*Fig 220    It is not, of course, a prerequisite of competion karate that you wait for your opponent to attack. From the same starting position as the previous technique it is possible to take the initiative by making a shuffle step to get in range...*

*Fig 223    If he continues to press his attack, hop back on the supporting leg, keeping the knee high, and time a mawashi-geri (roundhouse kick) to land just as he steps forwards...*

*Fig 224    ...then finish with an ura-mawashi-geri (hook kick) to the side of the jaw or neck.*

*Fig 225   Practising kicks on a slippery, wet rock is a traditional way of developing concentration and balance. Such training is potentially dangerous and should never be undertaken without a partner being present.*

# 5   Training Methods

*'Discipline is a state of mind, not just the process of training.'*
Bill Wallace

## A TRAINING PROGRAMME

Traditional karate training methods can be divided into three major groups: *kihon*, *kumite* and *kata*. Karate practice or training can take place two, three, five or even seven days a week, depending upon the enthusiasm and motivation of the trainee. It should be remembered that overtraining, placing excessive stress on the body and not allowing it sufficient time for rest, recovery and relaxation will result in progress being slower than it might be. Practice can, however, emphasize the study of tactics, strategy and technique without always entailing gruelling physical effort, so this too should be borne in mind.

Traditional Japanese training methods often totally disregard the effects and dangers of overtraining, regarding the whole process as *shugyo*, ascetic character training, which has of necessity to be *kurushi* (painful). The underlying philosophy is somewhat Nietzchean in flavour – 'that which does not kill us makes us stronger' – which is not always true, since some injuries can have life-long detrimental effects. There is no denying that the Spartan approach does produce some remarkably powerful and impressive karate champions, but the average trainee might do well to consider their own genetic potential before embarking on such a difficult and arduous path.

The average person can make good progress training three times a week and does not have to let his karate training become an obsession that takes over his life. Karate should be something that enriches and complements your life, not something that replaces it.

A typical modern two hour training session might be divided up in the following way:

- Warm up and stretching for general mobility for ten to fifteen minutes.
- Fifteen minutes practising *kihon*, blocking and punching, in static fashion and then moving up and down the dojo.
- A further fifteen minutes stretching to prepare the hips and legs for the following kicking practice.
- Fifteen minutes kicking, starting slowly and gradually building up to full intensity.
- Fifteen minutes doing five-, three- and one-step *kumite* in pairs.
- Fifteen minutes sparring.
- Fifteen minutes *kata*.
- Finally, fifteen minutes to warm down.

## KIHON (BASICS)

*Kihon* is the name given to the basic techniques of karate, and comprises stances, blocks, sweeps, kicks, punches and other striking techniques. The *kihon* are either practised individually with students arranged in lines, moving up and down the dojo by turns blocking, punching and kicking; or in pairs, with both students doing *ude-uchi-uke* against each other's forearms or, for example, both facing each other in *kiba-dachi*, one punching and the other blocking. *Kihon* are often practised to the sensei's count and may be as simple as doing a straightforward *oi-zuki* from one end of the dojo to another, then turning and doing the self same thing again in the opposite direction, or they can be quite involved. Combinations can be practised in this way, blocking, punching and kicking an imaginary opponent. The sensei might say: '*Jodan-age-uke*, *mae-geri-chudan*, *mawashi-geri-chudan*', finishing with '*gyaku-zuki-chudan*'. Or, in English: 'Rising head block, front kick to the midsection, roundhouse kick to the midsection, reverse punch to the midsection'. The variety of possible combinations is virtually endless. The important thing is to do them as if you were really fighting an opponent.

## *KUMITE* (SPARRING)

*Kumite* comprises a variety of different training methods, ranging from working with a partner in formalized, prearranged set-piece movements to the random unpredictability of free-sparring. The different types of *kumite* help to develop a sense of distance, timing and rhythm and quicken the reactions as you practise the techniques. Beginners usually learn *gohon kumite* first, which is a repetitive practice aimed at developing the timing and co-ordination necessary to make the basic techniques work. Typically, one partner will call out which technique he intends to do and what the target area is going to be. He might say '*Oizuki, jodan*', meaning that he intends to do a stepping punch to the face. Forewarned, the student receiving the attack is alert and waiting.

The person who called out the name of the technique will then attack with *oi-zuki* and the other will defend by stepping back and blocking. He will be attacked five times in total blocking each punch as it is thrown. The punches are usually blocked using the same technique each time to ensure that the trainee gets plenty of practice at doing the basic techniques. On the fifth attack, he will counter with a technique of his own. Normally, the roles are then reversed and the defender will take on the role of attacker, nominating his choice of technique and target area first and then attacking.

## *Sanbon Kumite* (Three Step Sparring)
*(Figs 226–230)*

Another form of *kumite* is *sanbon kumite*, where the number of attacks and blocks is reduced to three, the counter-attack coming after the third block.

*Fig 226   Both fighters begin in left free-fighting stance.*

*Fig 227   The attacker steps forward doing a right oi-zuki and the defender steps back making an inner block.*

*Fig 228   The attacker steps and punches again, but with left oi-zuki. The defender steps back and blocks again.*

*Fig 229    The attacker steps and punches, but is blocked...*

Obviously, brown and black belts should not be going flat out at white belts. The defender for his part should deliver a solid, effective block while remaining on balance at all times, and his counter attack should be instantaneous, allowing his partner no time to defend or evade. Stance must be correct and the technique must be delivered full power with focus and control to a specific target area, and should be accompanied by a *kiai* (spirit shout).

*Fig 230    ...and finally countered with gyaku-zuki.*

## *Ippon Kumite* (One Step Sparring)
### (Figs 231–233)

*Ippon kumite* is a kind of training that aims at sharpening up the student's reflexes; and speed even more. *Ippon kumite* involves immediately countering the first technique your opponent tries. Evasion and blocking movements are usually executed simultaneously with the counter technique. This is a good basis for training for competition, since it is usually the single attack or counter-attack which scores, and it allows the student to rehearse a number of standard situations. The attacker has to call out the target area and the intended technique and the defender will either defend with a technique picked by the instructor or with one of his own choice. The attacker should really try to land his technique, as only by going at full speed will he provide sufficient stimulus to make his partner do the same. The fact that he knows what is coming will give the defender just the edge he needs to block, provided there is no great difference in ability levels.

*Fig 231    Both karateka begin in left hanmi.*

*Fig 232    The attacker does jodan-oi-zuki and is blocked...*

*Fig 233    ...with age-uke and countered with gyaku-zuki.*

## *Jiyu-ippon-kumite* (semi-freestyle sparring)

The final form of *kumite* is *jiyu-ippon-kumite*, which amounts to semi-freestyle sparring. Rather than both partners standing still in *zenkutsu-dachi* to begin the exchange, they move around freely as in competition. The attacker names the technique he intends to use and the target area, but moves around trying to find a gap in his partner's defence or a lapse in his concentration. He attacks when he chooses. The defender's job is made more difficult because the attacker has the initiative as to when to attack, but he must try to exploit his opponent's intention to attack by feinting or feigning, apparently lowering his guard, deliberately moving into striking range and such like. The defender can use any block and counter technique he feels appropriate to the situation, and should aim to perform them simultaneously. This is difficult as a full-blooded attack is very difficult to block and requires great concentration, making the counter that little bit slower. The defender should aim however to make his counter-attack as instantaneous as possible.

## *Jiyu-Kumite* (Free-fighting)

The final stage in the *kumite* process is *jiyu-kumite*, which is free-fighting, or sparring. In training, the aim should be to concentrate on correct technique, speed and good control. More experienced fighters devise elaborate little sequences based on autogenics, which exploit fighters' natural reactions to certain feints to set them up for techniques. These can be quite subtle hand movements or shuffles of the feet, or may involve showing the opponent a technique, while really setting a trap for him. Quickly lifting and showing the knee to get the opponent to drop his guard in order to block what looks like the beginning of a *mae-geri* (front kick) to the stomach then switching the technique to *mawashi-geri* to the head is a good example of this. Some of the more subtle techniques for drawing or pulling an opponent, evolved by top fighters, only work on other top fighters – often the feints are too fast or complicated for less experienced fighters to understand the threat they pose, so they fail to react to them. In such cases, the top fighter simply has to return to basics, but it can be irritating to find that something which works on third and fourth dans is of no use with a brown belt or a first dan!

## DEFENCE AND COUNTERING

Often *ma-ai*, or distance, is what determines which techniques are appropriate counters to given attacks. Many beginners try to create space unnecessarily, to make their most practised techniques fit the situation. *Gyaku-zuki*, while a very useful and important technique does not always have to finish with the arm fully extended. Indeed, if you are too close to your opponent it is impractical, so it is important to experiment with the lesser-known and less-used punches such as *tate-zuki* and *ura-zuki*. Lateral movement is also useful, as is combination punching. In any effective combination the first attack must occupy the defender's attention and get a strong, definite reaction, make him step, duck or draw his block. The reaction can then be exploited.

## KATA

*Kata* are predetermined sequences of movements and techniques which have been handed down to the present day by the founders of the art, via their students. A combination of balletic movements, shadow boxing, breathing and dynamic tension exercises, the *kata* are the backbone of traditional karate and are said to contain the secrets of karate and the old masters' wisdom. Before free-sparring was introduced as a training method, *kata* was the main activity done in karate dojo. Some traditional styles would require students to practise a single *kata* many times a day every day for years before allowing them to progress to the next one. Many old masters criticize the modern trend of superficially learning dozens of *kata*, feeling it takes anything from ten to twenty years to master even the simplest ones. They may well be right, but such an attitude is typically Japanese in many other areas too. Japanese artists might paint the same scene a thousand times until they finally produce the perfect representation of what they see before them. Westerners have a different approach and there is a view that breadth of knowledge can be as important as depth of knowledge. The individual must make up his or her own mind.

Those styles with Buddhist links or spiritual tendencies often regard the *kata* as exercises in moving meditation. Even highly sports-oriented karateka tend to regard doing *kata* as a very important and a very valuable training method for improving balance, stance, fitness and general movement, not to mention learning the individual techniques and their applications. Although there are individual and team *kata* competitions, which are judged according to well established athletic and aesthetic standards, the real competition is with yourself. Really mastering a *kata* takes a lot of practice and a lot of repetition. Often, it is necessary to fathom the meaning of some of the movements, for they are not always obvious. Some beginners rush through *kata* training impatiently, because they fail to understand its importance and its value. It is no good imitating movements and not thinking about what they are for. Every part of a given *kata* has a reason for being included. Some good teachers do not explain fully the meaning of each technique or movement or breathing method in a *kata*, preferring to let the student learn by discovery. Never be afraid to ask your sensei to explain any part of a *kata* that you cannot understand, but be sure to choose the right moment. A verbal explanation sometimes helps students to grasp the meaning of particular movements and bring them alive. A dojo with mirror can be a big help in learning a *kata* as it allows the karateka to check his stances

and techniques even if there is no instructor present. Video is also an excellent training aid, because often what we think we do is not what we actually do, and video analysis after performance can allow us to be objective about what went well and what might be improved. This is of course true with reference to *kumite* also.

Because there are so many *kata*, their details varying from style to style and some of them consist of hundreds of complicated steps, blocks, kicks, strikes and stances. To describe them all is unfortunately beyond the scope of this book.

## WARMING UP

One of the most fundamental aspects of karate training is the warm-up. The aims of the warm-up are to prepare the body for the stress and strains of fighting by promoting strength, endurance and flexibility. After about ten minutes of calisthenics and stretching, the body is usually ready for the more strenuous, full speed, explosive movements required in karate practice. Older people generally take longer to warm up and it is important to take this into account when training. The importance of the warm-up as an essential component for promoting health and avoiding injury cannot be over-emphasised. It is very easy to pull or strain a muscle, or damage ligaments or tendons by going straight into combat, whether in training or competition, without warming up and stretching.

## Callisthenics and Stretching

The basic callisthenics and stretching undertaken in a karate class are intended to warm up the body immediately and prepare it for the shocks and stresses of combat and, in the long term, to improve the students' strength, endurance and flexibility. Normally, the various joints of the body are mobilized and muscles are stretched and lengthened to prevent stiffness and tension which would

# Stretching Exercises for Hip, Leg and Lower Back Flexibility
*(Figs 234–241)*

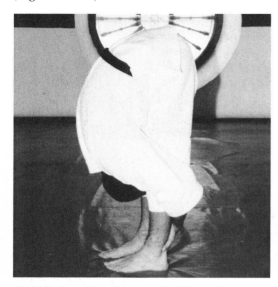

*Fig 235    Backwards bends for the groins and lower back.*

*Fig 234    Forward bends promote flexibility in the hamstrings, hips and lower back. Standing in a relaxed upright position breathe in, then, keeping the knees locked straight, bend forwards at the hips until your chest touches your front thighs. Slowly breathe out as you reach the fully stretched position which you should hold from five to seven seconds, then return to the upright position and breathe in again. All of the exercises demonstrated here should be done in the same slow, controlled fashion, paying particular attention to breathing. Whenever a particular muscle group feels tight, exhale and consciously relax it as you do so.*

*Fig 238    This action prepares hips and legs for kicking.*

*Fig 240    Once warmed up, take the chest to the knee.*

*Fig 237    The shiko or wide-legged sumo squat opens the hip joints.*

*Fig 236    Sitting tailor fashion stretches the inner thighs.*

*Fig 239    Full box splits is an advanced movement that not all trainees can reach.*

*Fig 241    For the extremely flexible athlete, the splits position can be further extended by taking the chest to the floor.*

slow the karateka down. Exercises like press-ups and sit-ups are also performed to get the heart and lungs working and to pump oxygen around the system, waking up the body at the same time as the muscles are strengthened.

There are a number of different techniques for improving flexibility; different types of stretching that can produce good results. The important thing to remember is not to exceed your limitations. People vary greatly in terms of the range of movement of their joints and the elasticity of their muscles. Some general guidelines are: warm up slowly, especially in cold weather, and never bounce. Do not hold your breath, but inhale as you prepare to stretch and exhale as you make the stretching movement.

## Static Stretching

The majority of stretching done in karate dojo is passive static stretching. That is to say that the karateka uses bodyweight, or is assisted by a partner to reach a stretched position and holds it. Doing the splits or having a partner lift your leg up in the air on his shoulder as far as it can go, are examples of this kind of stretching.

The stretch is usually held anything from five seconds to a minute depending upon ability. Active static stretching is considerably more difficult because it involves placing a limb in a stretched position purely by muscular tension. Lifting the leg into a side-kick position and holding the foot out at head height is an example of this type of stretching which can also be used to improve balance and strength.

## Isometric stretching

Isometric stretching is the quickest way to improve flexibility, but in terms of the effect it has on muscles, it is the most strenuous. It makes use of a technique called neuromuscular proprioceptive facilitation, and is especially effective when done with a partner. Basically, the stretched position is reached but then the stretched muscle is tensed for eight to ten seconds, in isometric fashion, then the tension is relaxed and the muscle can be stretched a little further. The initial stretched position does not have to be the trainee's absolute limit. A practical application would be for one trainee to lift another's foot on his shoulder until the hamstring begins to stretch. Once the stretch is felt, the other trainee should contract the muscles in the back of the leg and try to push down as hard as he can. He will not be able to move his partner, and so the muscle cannot contract or shorten, which is what isometric training means – muscular effort without movement. When he stops tensing and relaxes the muscle, there is a reflex relaxing action in the muscle which then allows it to be stretched a little further. The partner lifts the leg a little higher and the process is repeated. The range of movement can be increased up to five times, alternating legs, but this type of stretching should not be repeated until forty-eight hours have elapsed and the muscles have had time to recover, although gentle static stretching can be done in the interim.

## Dynamic stretching

Dynamic stretching is considered by many to be a misnomer, since it involves the demonstration of flexibility, rather than its development. Rapid movements to fully stretched positions are known to result in an automatic protection mechanism known as a stretch reflex, which eventually shortens the range of the muscle. Exercises that fall into this category, such as high leg swings, should only be done when the muscles have already been safely and fully stretched, in which case the dynamic movements will not take the muscle to full extension, and the negative effects of the stretch reflex can be avoided. The high leg swings done in karate warm-ups should not be introduced before stretching groins, hips and hamstrings with passive static stretching techniques first.

# CONDITIONING METHODS

## Traditional Okinawan Training Methods

Okinawan styles of karate place great emphasis on developing strength in the hands and grip, and a variety of mechanisms and training devices have been developed to achieve this. Mastery of *kiba-dachi*, the horse riding stance, is a vital prerequisite of these methods, so trainees in *Te* often spend up to two hours at a time holding the stance, and developing great isometric strength and flexibility in the legs and hips.

### Training Equipment

In the Goju-Ryu style *sanchin dachi* is frequently used for walking up and down the dojo while carrying heavy stone jars, called *kame*, using the hands like claws to grip the rims. These could be filled with sand, water, or even lead shot depending on the level of the trainee. This exercise makes the shoulders and forearms burn and develops a powerful grip.

One training device used in Okinawan systems is the *makiage gu*, a kind of wall-mounted wrist roller, consisting of a wooden rack with a revolving wooden bar in the centre to which a rope is attached. A weight is tied to the end of the rope and it can be slowly wound up and unwound to work the hands, wrists and forearms. Another device is the *chirakairishi*, or power stone (also called *chishi*). These take various forms, but usually consist of a wooden handle and a circular stone. Sometimes they have the stone in the middle and they are used like a swingbell ; or the stone may be at one end and the device and used like a heavy stone hammer to develop strength in the shoulders, forearms and wrists. Stone weights called *sashi* are also used to strengthen the muscles used in punching and blocking, and *tetsugeta*, iron clogs based on the traditional Japanese geta, wooden clogs worn with two toed socks, are used

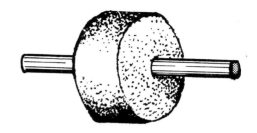

*Fig 242   A chishi or power stone.*

to strengthen the muscles of the legs and hips for kicking, just as western gymnasts and bodybuilders use iron boots, and ankle and wrist weights.

A more interesting machine is a sort of *makiwara* with a weighted lever. Basically, it is a post wrapped in straw with a lever attached. The trainee has to catch the lever, gripping it as if it were an adversary's wrist or jacket. Pulling on the lever offers a resistance similar to the weight of a human body because of the weight on the other end. The trainee then kicks or strikes the post with an open-handed blow. Some schools use a heavy, iron hoop, about five feet in diameter, and oval shaped. They train with it by standing it up and pushing it to a partner, who has to catch it, prevent it from falling and push it back.

Finally, one of the most gruelling training drills used on Okinawa is known as *kanshu*, and is used to condition the hands. *Kanshu* means 'penetrating hand' and derives from Chinese training methods called 'the iron fist' or 'iron palm'. It involves filling a receptacle with powder and repeatedly plunging the hand into it using straight-fingered strikes. The contents are periodically changed for something harder, progressing through rice, sand, beans and finally pebbles, until the hands become fully conditioned.

These methods while apparently primitive have helped to produce karateka with exceptional speed, strength physical endurance and toughness, so they should not be disparaged by those who have not trained with them. Newer does not always mean better.

*Fig 243　Sensei Higaonna leads a group of karateka in the use of chirakairishi or 'power stones' on a Goju-Ryu training course. Photograph by Tim Green.*

## Modern Weight Training Methods

Sheer strength is relevant in karate only to the extent that it can be expressed as speed (power), and the effectiveness of any explosive movements is determined by a variety of other factors, including flexibility, relaxation and motor co-ordination. Most martial artists, though, at some time or other come to the conclusion that their techniques could be more powerful, and often turn to weight training as the solution. There are many people who do karate two or three times a week and have no desire to do any other form of physical training. That is perfectly acceptable for recreational karateka, who do karate as a hobby to keep themselves fit, flexible and ready and aware of how to defend themselves if attacked. There are many competitive young karateka, however, who burn with the desire to do better, and they can make great improvements by intelligent additional training with weights. Others simply cannot get to the dojo as often as they would like to because of other commitments, but may have access to a gymnasium, and free time in their lunch hour, which they wish to put to better use.

Strength is always comparative. In calculating your strength you have to consider your power to weight ratio, which relates your performance to your bodyweight. A 70kg (150lb) man who can lift 100kg (220lb) is relatively stronger than a 95kg (210lb) man who can lift 120kg (254lb), even though the heavier man has greater absolute strength. Your maximum in an exercise refers to the maximum amount of weight you can lift unassisted for a single repetition. Training poundages are then calculated as percentages of your maximum for given training effects, such as increasing endurance, speed or sheer strength.

An extremely important consideration in competition karate is strength endurance. Two karateka may be of equal strength at the beginning of a training session or contest, but if one is much fitter than the other he may seem, and to all intents and purposes he will be, that much stronger than the other as the fight or training goes on, outlasting him and wearing him down. This can even be the case when one of the fighters is initially a lot stronger than the other, since strength levels can fluctuate in the course of a contest. Large muscles and a high proportion of white twitch fibres can be tremendously powerful, but those muscles have to be supplied with oxygen via the blood in order for them to keep working, which is where heart and lung fitness becomes so important. Bigger muscle groups burn energy at a faster rate, so fighters with large muscles may be difficult to overpower, but they can be worn down by fitter opponents. Strength endurance can be improved by aerobic training and weights circuits. Sheer power can best be increased by heavy weight training, sprinting and pylometric training.

The karateka going into a gymnasium in order to weight train is likely to encounter all sorts of conflicting theories and information. Most gyms are run with a bias towards either bodybuilding or fitness so it is absolutely vital to know why you want to do weight training. Do you want to increase your endurance, your absolute strength (punching and kicking power) or do you want to lose bodyfat and develop greater speed? The type and quantity of training you do will vary as much as the objectives themselves.

Many of the terms and concepts used in training are used very loosely so for the purpose of clarity, before embarking on a weight training programme it is important to define your goals and to be clear about the meaning of the terminology you hear and use.

## Body building

Body building techniques are designed to increase muscle volume, density and size. Bodybuilders are not usually too concerned about getting faster or stronger, they want to gain muscle and lose fat for the most part. They often do lift very heavy weights, because a bigger muscle is usually a stronger muscle. A bodybuilder not using steroids (which are illegal and dangerous and should never be taken except on medical prescription for certain illnesses) will consider himself to have made excellent progress if he is able to put on 2.5–3kg of muscle (6–7lb) in a year.

People who claim to put on half a stone in six weeks usually do so by eating more and cutting back on aerobic activity, like running. They do put on weight, but for the most part it is fat and water that is retained in the muscle. They usually do feel stronger, however, because of the change in their training and diet, and the extra mass adds weight to their techniques. The acid test is whether they can increase their weight and get faster, which is not very common.

## Devising a Programme

Repetition is central to all martial arts, and it is the basis of weight training too; but recovery, rest and nutrition are equally important. It is not advisable for the karateka to weight train every day because the muscles need at least forty-eight hours to recover from high intensity weight training, and sometimes much longer. A strong, but untrained man unwise enough to do a heavy squatting session is likely to suffer from painful lactic acid muscle stiffness in the legs for up to five or six days after the actual session. This is a clear indication that the trainee has overdone it. If you are new to weight training or are returning after a lay off, always spend the first two weeks handling only moderate poundages, to allow the muscles and joints to get used to the exercises. The muscles must be given a chance to recover between training sessions, and the trainee must eat at least a gram of protein for every kilo of bodyweight, to ensure that the muscle tissue broken down in training is repaired and rebuilt. If doing karate three times a week and weight training three times a week there is a very good chance of overtraining. A good compromise is to do two karate sessions and three weight training sessions in one week, rest the weekends and alternate the following week doing three karate sessions and two weight training sessions.

We are all different and some people thrive on programmes that simply run others into the ground. Genetics, too, play an important part, some people get bigger and stronger doing relatively little training, while for others it is much harder. It is up to the individual to experiment to find out what works for them. Of course, a good coach or trainer can save you from wasting time going down blind alleys, advising and monitoring progress and difficulties. A good training partner is priceless and you can help to motivate each other and get feedback on the after-effects of training sessions – which exercises seem to be working, how to get more out of the sessions and generally make the whole process more fun.

## The Set System

For the beginner there is a bewildering variety of exercises and training systems to choose from. The set system is the basis of all modern weight training programmes and allows for considerable flexibility in terms of tailoring a programme to meet specific needs.

In any given weight training session, the amount of work done should be broken up into sets of repetitions. The advantage weight training has over callisthenics is that the intensity (i.e. the amount of resistance) of the exercise can be altered, rather than just the duration and recovery period. For example, suppose that a trainee aiming to develop his shoulders, chest and triceps and who is used to doing fifty press-ups in his karate class, decides to do fifty repetitions of bench press. If he chooses a weight light enough to allow him to do forty consecutive repetitions, say 30kg if he has a maximum single lift of 90kg, it would probably have little effect in increasing his actual strength and be useful only as an endurance exercise. Instead, he can opt to lift a heavier weight and break the number of repetitions down into sets. He could lift 60kg for ten repetitions, rest for two minutes and repeat the process, doing four sets of ten in total. By doing this he has doubled the amount of work done, although the recovery periods have naturally increased the time taken to do the exercises.

When strength training it is important to allow sufficient time for recovery between sets, otherwise the muscle simply does not recover sufficiently to work at the desired intensity; the muscle has to be pushed to failure by the last set, and not taking a long enough rest period will mean failure occurs much earlier. Resting between sets is sometimes a difficult concept for people trained in martial arts to grasp, especially if they are used to doing circuit training, where the aim is to keep the heart and lungs working and not rest between sets. When training for strength, the breathing is normally under control after a minute's rest, and so they tend to feel ready to do the next set. It is important to wait, a minimum of two or, where very heavy poundages are being handled, three minutes. This gives the muscle the time it needs to recover and allows for heavier weights to be handled and greater strength gains to be made. Resting less than three minutes will mean the muscle does not recover sufficiently to make efforts of near maximum intensity.

## Progression

This is an important principle. After two weeks of training three times per week, doing four sets of ten repetitions with 60kg (132lb), increase the weight to 70kg (155lb) and do five sets of eight. The total number of repetitions is the same, but the total work done is increased by almost 17 per cent. The following two weeks could see the weight increased to 75 or 80kg (165 or 175lb) and the repetitions reduced to six sets of six.

A partner should always be on hand to spot when heavy weights are being handled and, if necessary, to assist with the final repetitions when the trainee's muscles may become temporarily exhausted and need a little help to complete the set. This six week spell could be followed by a week's rest from weight training, then another six week spell would begin but with a starting weight 5kg (11lb) heavier than the last. Consider the following progressive loadings:

| | |
|---|---|
| 4 sets of 10 with 60kg = | 2,400kg |
| 5 sets of 8 with 70kg = | 2,800kg |
| 6 sets of 6 with 80kg = | 2,880kg |
| 4 sets of 10 with 65kg = | 2,600kg |
| 5 sets of 8 with 75kg = | 3,000kg |
| 6 sets of 6 with 85kg = | 3,060kg |

This would be an excellent progression over a twelve-to-thirteen week period, after which the trainee could do a strength test to check his progress. If able to do 6sets of 6 with 85kg (188lb) he would surely be able to do 100kg (220lb) for a single repetition; a 10kg (22lb) improvement on his original personal best. This is just a sample model, but indicates the principles of progressive resistance and overload. It is important to bear in mind that the human body is not a machine, and that there may be considerable fluctuations in energy levels and ability to perform from one session to another. There may be sessions when you simply cannot lift as much or do as many reps as you had planned to for a variety of reasons. Occasionally feeling like this is nothing to worry about, but if every training session sees you failing to meet your targets, you are either overtrained or simply being unrealistic in your goals. Planned workloads should be reasonable and achievable in order for the training to be enjoyable.

The lower reps with the heavier weights constitute the most effective form of strength training, but the rep variety, especially for karateka who do not train with weights all year round, also has a beneficial effect and is a lot less monotonous than trying to do six sets of six over a three month period, only trying to increase the weights lifted.

## Circuit Training

Circuit training using light weights (less than 50 per cent of the maximum) for high repetitions (twenty to forty) will have a marked effect on local muscular endurance, but will not increase absolute strength or speed. Many athletes also make the mistake of thinking that because a weight is light, they should move it as quickly as possible. They fall into the trap of using ballistic, swinging motions with the result that the muscle is not worked throughout its full range of movement, or that the wrong muscles are exercised. In the case of barbell curls, an exercise which when performed correctly trains the biceps muscles, cheating by swinging the weight (which is technique used to good effect by trained bodybuilders to increase the intensity of the work done by the biceps) when done by a karateka, simply means that the lower back and shoulders do the work and the training effect on the biceps is minimal.

It is true to say in running that the faster you go, the more energy you use. Sprinting 100 metres, for instance, engages the body's anaerobic system and the muscles work flat out, deriving their energy from stored glycogen rather than from the body's aerobic system. This is not the case in weight training, however, where light weights are being handled in loose fashion. The muscles have to contract really quickly when maximum heavy weights are being handled, such as when doing a clean and jerk with weights of about 80 to 95 per cent of the maximum. If the exercise is not performed at high speed using all the explosive power you can muster, you will simply fail to lift the weight. Ten repetitions with body weight will leave most karateka breathless and unable to continue the exercise because heavy weights place a huge demand on the body's anaerobic system. The training effect with light weights, when performing high repetitions, is solely aerobic and doing the exercises faster often just means that the training is made easier. If you are a knockdown fighter doing Kyokushinkai and opt to do high repetition weights circuits, you will be able to hit just as hard for longer, but you will not necessarily hit any harder or faster. Such training can make you fitter and able to endure longer than your opponent, so it has its place.

It is important to be clear about what you want from your weight training regime. Full contact and knockdown karate require different physical preparation programmes than semi-contact does. All karateka need speed and endurance (not always easy qualities to develop at the same time), but contact fighters need to develop greater power besides of course resilience to being struck, too. In order to increase speed, the weights handled should be between 50 and 80 per cent of your maximum in a given exercise. The exercises in the 50 to 80 per cent of maximum range should be performed with slow, deliberate movements; it is neither necessary nor desirable to lift weights fast in order to increase speed. Slow movement with continuous tension on the muscles involved is the correct training speed, say a second and a half to lift the weight, and up to three seconds to lower it.

Training poundages are usually calculated as a percentage of the maximum weight a trainee can lift for a single repetition in a given exercise. If you are capable of a 136kg (300lb) bench press for one repetition and want to get even stronger you would need to train in the 80 to 95 per cent range 109–130kg (240 to 285lb) doing from six to three reps, depending on the weight chosen. When calculating poundages for a particular training effect the following should be borne in mind:

1 The white twitch muscle fibres, which are responsible for explosive movement, are best activated by training with weights in the 80 to 95 per cent of maximum range. Training with weights of this magnitude leads to increases in speed in conjunction with strength.

2 Training with weights of 95 per cent of maximum and upwards develops strength only and is potentially the most dangerous type of training as it is the most likely to result in injury. Only one or two repetitions are possible with such weights, and such specialised training is best left to the powerlifters and Olympic weight lifters.

3 Training with weights that range from 50 to 80 per cent of the maximum primarily develops speed.

4 Training with less than 50 per cent of your maximum will only develop stamina and not absolute strength or speed.

The most important thing then for the semi-contact/sport karate fighter to realize is that weight training can make him faster as well as stronger, so its importance may be greater than is often believed.

It is worth bearing in mind that athletes in other sports do much of their weight training in the off season, to get themselves strong and prepared for the competitive season. Karate is not practised in a seasonal fashion, but continues all year round with no rest seasons. Consequently, a three-month block of weight training is most appropriate to the karateka and might best be undertaken in what corresponds to the off season in other sports. If the karateka has an important competition or grading in the spring, then the time to do the weight training is through the winter. By raising his strength threshold, and giving himself time to adjust to his new strength levels and incorporate any strength improvements into his skill training, the karateka will be much better prepared for competition.

Heavy weight training should cease at least six weeks before a major competition – some teachers say up three months before! Others advocate strength training once a week right up until the week before the competition so as not to lose the gains made. One thing is certain: on the day of a contest the karateka must go out feeling fit, sharp, rested, injury free and raring to go, not worn out from being over-trained.

## Weight Training Exercises for Karate

There is a large selection of weight training exercises that can be used to strengthen virtually any muscle in the body. Even a relatively small muscle like the biceps in the arm has a host of different exercises that can be used to train it, such as: barbell curls, preacher curls, concentration curls with dumb bells, alternate arm curls, seated dumb bell curls on inclined bench, hammer curls, and so on. It is not necessary to try and do all of these exercises every time you go into the gym, in fact it would be impossible. Select one or two exercises per muscle group at the most and move on to the next body part. It is generally a good idea to train the larger muscle groups first, as these use up the most energy and it is best to work them when you are fresh. If you find that it is too difficult to do a whole body work out three times a week and practise karate try doing chest and back on Monday, legs on Wednesday and shoulders and arms on Friday.

Before selecting which exercises to include in a weight training programme for karate, it is best to consider the biomechanical nature of the sport and its requirements. The vast variety of exercises fall into the following seven categories which describe their usefulness to karateka.:upper body pushing (arms straightening), upper body pulling (arms bending), leg and hip extension (legs straightening), hamstring work (leg bending), calf work (ankle flexion), lower back strengthening and abdominal strengthening.

Pushing power is needed for punching and blocking, pulling power is used to pull back the opposite arm when punching, leg work is necessary for kicking, lower back and abdominal work is important in helping to avoid injuries. Karateka are inclined to do a lot of sit-ups and leg raises in order to condition their abdomens, but often neglect to strengthen the lower back in complementary fashion, which often, sooner or later, leads to hip and lower back problems.

Generally one exercise for each of these seven functions should be sufficient, but in order to maintain variety in the programme it can be good idea to change the individual exercises fairly regularly. Remember:

• Power training: 80 to 95 per cent of maximum, six sets of six repetitions
• Speed training: 50 to 80 per cent of maximum, three sets of eight to ten repetitions
• Endurance: below 50 per cent of maximum three to six sets of twenty to forty repetitions.

In all cases good exercise form should be observed. Cheating techniques, swinging the weight or bouncing should be avoided as they are potentially dangerous. Do not sacrifice proper form for the sake of heavier poundages. Interesting routines can be tailor made selecting from the following 41 basic exercises (there are many more!)

If training legs once or twice a week you might choose to do a pyramid on the squat then three sets of ten on each exercise. Lunges done holding dumb-bells in the hands or a bar across the chest or shoulders are worthy of special attention for the karate competitor. If you wanted to do chest and back or shoulders and arms on different days, the same system applies. To do a whole body work-out you can select one or two exercises from each group and put them together using the appropriate combination of sets, reps, poundages and rest periods, depending on whether you want to train for speed, endurance or power.

| Explosive power | Triceps |
|---|---|
| Power clean | Triceps extensions |
| Split jerk | French press |
| Clean and jerk | Push downs |
| Dead lift | Parallel bar dips |
| **Chest and back** | Close grip bench |
| Bench press | press |
| Incline press | **Forearms** |
| Flyes | Wrist roller |
| Seated rowing | Wrist curl |
| Bent over rowing | Reverse curl |
| Pull downs | **Lower back and** |
| Chins | **Hamstrings** |
| Pull overs | Back raises |
| **Leg exercises** | Stiff leg dead lift |
| Lunges | Leg curl |
| Squats | **Shoulders** |
| Leg press | Seated press |
| Leg extensions | Lateral raises |
| Leg curls | Upright rowing |
| Calf raises | Shrugs |
| **Biceps** | **Abdominals and** |
| Barbell curl | **Hip flexors** |
| Preacher curl | Inclined sit ups |
| Hammer curl | Inclined leg raises |
| Seated dumb-bell curl | Crunches |
| Concentration curl. | |

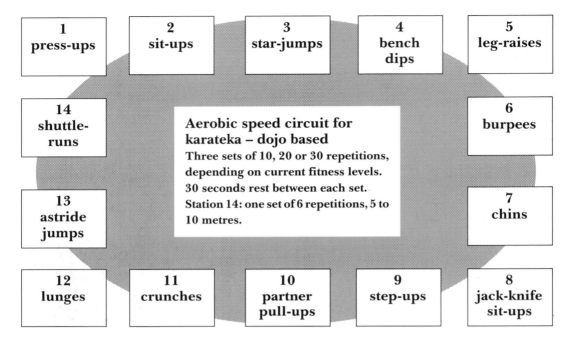

*Fig 244   A dojo based aerobic callisthenics training circuit designed to increase overall speed and strength endurance.*

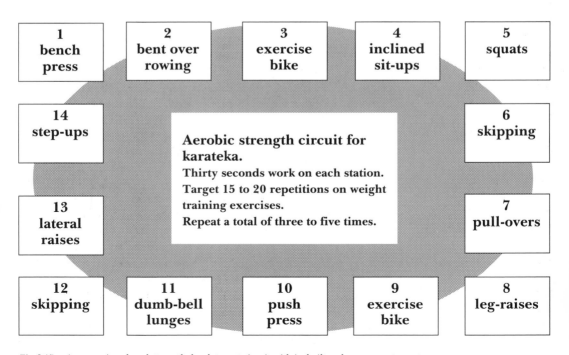

*Fig 245   A gymnasium-based strength development circuit with in-built endurance component.*

130

## *KIME* (FOCUS TRAINING)

*Kime*, or focus, is a vital part of karate training. The aim is to channel all of the body's force into a single decisive, destructive blow. In the case of a forefist strike, all of the body's power – the drive from the legs, the turning of the hips and the strength of the shoulders chest back and arm muscles – is focused into the striking area, made up of the two large knuckles of the index and middle fingers. A well-focused blow does not just strike at a target, it strikes through it. In training kicks and punches are pulled so as not to inflict damage on training partners. In real combat though a punch to the jaw should be aimed through to the back of the adversary's head.

The traditional training device for developing focus was the *makiwara*, a wooden post driven into the ground and covered with straw. Many students use the *makiwara* to condition the wrists and hands, punching it until the knuckles are grazed and bleeding, session after session, until eventually an ugly callus forms. This is generally felt to be unnecessary by modern day karateka, some of whom regard it as an abuse. The real value of *makiwara* training is in the practice it affords for developing hip rotation when striking or kicking. However, some young people in particular often have an immature desire to let other people know that they do karate, and the calluses are often proudly, if somewhat naively, displayed as an indication of their toughness. Some dojo have wall-mounted striking pads that can be used in similar fashion to the *makiwara* for developing focus and accuracy.

## EQUIPMENT FOR DEVELOPING STRIKING SKILLS

### Focus Gloves and Pads

Sport karate exponents have taken a leaf out of the professional boxers' book and make greater use of focus gloves and pads than they do of the *makiwara* especially for punching. The focus pad or glove is good for simulating head shots, as it is

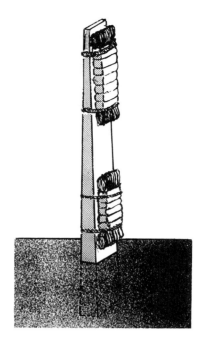

*Fig 246   The makiwara, the traditional training aid for developing effective karate techniques.*

more or less the same size as a head and can be moved and held in different positions to train the karateka's reflexes and preparedness to use different punches. If the skill level is high enough, kicks too can be trained in this way.

### The Heavy Bag

This is used more for developing power, by full contact and knockdown fighters. Straight punches, hooks, roundhouse kicks and front kicks to the bottom of the bag (for self defence use only) can all be usefully practised, normally in two- or three-minute bursts, duplicating the round duration of their respective sports. All karateka should take the time to do some heavy bag work to get an idea of what it feels like to hit something full power, as well as to get an idea of the effectiveness of their techniques.

## Punch Balls

Punch balls, either suspended floor to ceiling by rubber bands, or wall-mounted, are additional useful training aids for developing timing and accuracy as well as cardiovascular fitness.

## Rubber Bands

Rubber bands tied to wall bars can be used for providing variable resistance for punching exercises. The trainee can stand with his back to the wall and punch against the contractile force of the band, or he can face the wall bars and pull the band on his hip, then punch using the assistance of the snap and pull of the band to accelerate the speed of his punch.

## Focus Shields
*(Figs 247–248)*

*Fig 247   Practising ashi-barai with the focus shield allows the sweeper to use more power without injuring his partner.*

Focus shields are used mainly for kicking practice, and are very useful for developing power and snap in your kicks. They are also useful to assist beginners and intermediate level karateka with their accuracy, especially for techniques like back kick, which are difficult to do on a bag. The flat surface area makes the shield easier to hit, and the foot is less likely to skid off it than it is off a bag.

*Fig 248   The focus shield can be used to develop dynamic kicking power with techniques such as ushiro-geri, mawashi-geri and, as here, yoko-geri-kekomi.*

## *TAMESHIWARI* (**BREAKING**)

Breaking demonstrations, where karate experts break bricks with a knife hand strike, kick through boards and smash piles of roof tiles with their heads, are part of the popular conception of what karate is. It is in fact only a tiny part of the modern activity. Many of today's modern sport karate stars find the subject tiresome and boring and would like to get right away from the sort of primitive bash and smash image of karate that they feel it projects! Breaking, or *tameshiwari*, is more representative of Korean karate-like sys-

tems such as Taekwondo, than Okinawan or Japanese karate. It is, however undertaken in many schools, principally to demonstrate the power and effectiveness of the techniques, which are never used in actual combat because of the danger of injury.

Breaking also helps give students confidence in the power of their own techniques, which they may otherwise lack if they have never used a technique actually to hit an opponent.

There are a number of elements to consider in breaking, such as conditioning, skill, concentration, focus and choice of material.

*Fig 249   Tameshiwari or breaking to test the effectiveness of techniques is practised in many styles of karate. Here karate, judo and ju-jitsu expert Errol Field, breaks a stack of roofing tiles.*

## Selecting Materials

When selecting materials to break, whether for training or demonstration purposes some care must be taken. The range of things which can be broken is incredible: bricks, bottles, blocks of ice, baseball bats, wooden boards, tiles, kerb stones and breeze blocks, to name but a few. The range of techniques that can be used to break these things is equally diverse. Kyokushinkai exponents break baseball bats by kicking them with their shins, which is a fairly effective way of communicating to an audience that when they shin kick each other in the legs, the reason that they do not fall down is that they are very well conditioned, not that their kicks are ineffective. In any breaking attempt, the person most likely to be injured if anything goes wrong is the one attempting the break.

### Wood

Beginners usually learn to break wooden boards first, although it can be less expensive in the long run to buy re-usable plastic breaker-boards which are designed to 'break' if hit correctly. Most trainees feel that breaking wood is more satisfying, however, because of the natural quality of the material and precisely because wooden boards are not designed to break!.

When breaking wood for a demonstration it is advisable to select something hard and strong but which can be broken by a high-impact strike. The point of the demonstration is usually to indicate the power of karate techniques so there is no point breaking flimsy materials that the average member of the audience could break without training. When wooden boards are used, it is always best to check the grain and make certain that you break the wood with the grain. Attempting to break wood against the grain is a completely different proposition, which can result in considerable embarrassment, not to mention physical injury. The type of wood chosen is im-

*Fig 250   Frank Perry, 6th dan Kyokushinkai, shows the awesome power that can be generated by top karateka.*

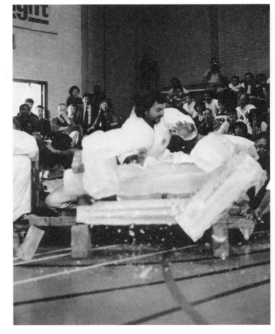

*Fig 253   ...and the bottom two blocks remained intact.*

*Fig 251   Performing an ice break is no easy task and here the unevenness of the blocks added to the difficulty.*

*Fig 252   Breaking does not always go according to plan. The first two blocks broke cleanly, but the spacers slipped...*

*Fig 254   A second strike was required to finish the job. What the uninitiated should realize is...*

*Fig 255   ...that such obstacles simply demonstrate the genuine difficulty involved in attempting such feats.*

portant too. It is best to select a wood with little tensile strength, which is fairly rigid and does not give or flex. Thickness is usually an indication of strength, but it is considerably easier to break a stack of three one-inch boards with an inch of space between each than it is to break three boards, one on top of the other with no space. A single three-inch thick board is much stronger than three one-inch boards and such thick boards are not often attempted, even by experts.

Some materials are notoriously difficult to break, even in thin sheets. Plywood, because it is made up of interlaced, crossed grains, which makes it extremely springy and flexible, should never be chosen, because it simply will not break. White pine, prana pine and chip board are suitable for breaking because they break cleanly, but hardwoods such as teak and mahogany ought to be avoided by all but the most skilled as their density makes it more likely that the bones of the hands and feet break before the wood does. In fact, house bricks, despite being much thicker, are easier to break than some hardwoods.

## Bricks

Care has to be taken breaking bricks. The average house brick is made of clay, and will have been baked in a high temperature oven to harden it; but not all bricks are the same. A darker coloured, slightly heavier engineering brick, which looks almost the same as the typical house brick is much much stronger and is virtually impossible to break without using a hammer.

The physics involved in breaking a brick are straightforward, and the whole process has been measured scientifically a number of times. With both ends of the brick placed on a suitable base, such as a couple of other bricks a force of between 225 and 450kg (500 and 1,000lb) will bend the brittle material to its elastic limit (which will be something less than a millimetre, depending upon the temperature at which it was fired) causing it to fracture from the base upwards.

The most effective way to apply this force is to focus it into the smallest possible area, hence the popularity of the knife hand, which focuses and transmits the kinetic energy of the blow through the relatively small surface area of the side of the hand. Using a back hand or palm heel increases the surface area of the strike, considerably adding to the difficulty of the break. An unconditioned hand in either case – even if the person delivering the strike is capable of generating the force necessary to break the brick – will deform on impact, spreading to absorb the energy of the collision, usually causing injury to the hand or wrist. No one should attempt to break a brick without going through an extended hand-conditioning programme in preparation.

Breaking should be a test of skill as well as conditioning. Weightlifters, shot-putters and boxers are also capable of breaking wooden boards just by applying sheer power and blasting through the target. If the thickness, or quantity of boards is increased, however, they rapidly reach a point where they hurt their hands and fail to break the boards.

Skilled karateka perform a staggering variety of impressive, at times almost unbelievable, breaks with a wide variety of techniques. The techniques used are all combat effective, otherwise there is no point in doing the break. They usually range from the relatively easy elbow strikes, forefist and knife hands to the much more difficult, jumping spinning kicks and spear hand strikes.

As well as being a good way of demonstrating the effectiveness of karate techniques, breaking can also be a good form of training to develop speed, focus and timing. As well as breaking stationary, supported objects, advanced trainees can perform suspended strikes and even air breaks. Focus has to be perfect for these breaks to work. A suspended strike can involve hanging a board by a piece of string from the ceiling and breaking it as it hangs. Air breaks are the most difficult of all and involve throwing things into the air and breaking them in mid-air. Top experts can throw a board into the air and do a jumping spinning reverse roundhouse or back kick and break the board in mid-air, an incredible feat of co-ordination, skill and precision timing. Suspended strikes and air breaks require great speed as well as power, otherwise the target will not break. In breaking terms they are the supreme test of technique and focus.

It is easier to generate the power necessary to break using the feet, because the legs and hips are so much stronger than the arms and shoulders. The feet need relatively little conditioning, since they are designed with a built-in stress-bearing function. On the negative side, for the beginner at least, accuracy and focus are more difficult to achieve with the feet than with the hands.

## Conditioning

The role played by conditioning in many breaking techniques should not be underestimated. The ball of the foot, the heel and the elbow are naturally hard striking areas, the hands, fingers and toes are not. Time has to be spent strengthening and conditioning these parts of the body. Even the shins can be conditioned to the point where they can break a baseball bat, but it is a long, slow process and inevitably involves some degree of pain and discomfort.

Conditioning should be done with low intensity and often. Many trainees do press-ups on their knuckles to assist in forming a solid fist and to strengthen their wrists. The makiwara can be used for the same purpose. The *kanshu* method has already been described, and some karateka practise at home by striking bundles of newspaper, and even telephone directories, lightly and repeatedly to condition fingers and hands.

Whichever method you choose, the important thing is to avoid injury and keep safety in mind. Some karateka do no hand conditioning because they fear problems with arthritis later in life. There is currently no conclusive evidence of a definite connection between the two.

*Fig 256  Although training with focus shields develops good power and focus it does not condition the feet for breaking. Using the instep mawashi-geri for kicking is popular in competition and training, but where breaking is concerned the instep is a fragile structure made up of small, not very strong bones which are easily damaged by striking hard, unyielding surfaces.*

*Safety Tip*
**Beginners should never at any time attempt to break on their own initiative, but should seek out a competent instructor who can take them through the necessary conditioning processes and ensure that they are adequately prepared to do breaking.**

# 6  Sport Karate

*'Ge koku jo'*
*'Those below overcome those above'*

*Ge koku jo* is a phrase used by Japanese historians to describe the tumultuous sixteenth century in Japan, a time of virtually uninterrupted civil war which saw a succession of samurai families, clans, houses and alliances seize power only to have it torn from their grasp by the next generation of hungry *bushi* emerging from the lower classes of the military elite. This period of interminable strife known as the time of the warring states, finally came to an end with the establishment of the Tokugawa Shogunate in 1603.

The applications of the phrase *Ge koku jo* are numerous. In traditional karate it is a reminder to those who train in martial arts that they must never give up in their efforts to improve, because there is always fresh blood coming through. For the beginner or intermediate student in sport karate, it is an inspiring thought, giving students the idea that they may one day overcome people who can beat them at present and even become masters themselves. Likewise, those people who have become champions and are at the top must constantly keep in mind that there will always be challengers, eager to take them on and beat them, in order to become champions themselves.

## PSYCHOLOGY OF COMPETITION

The sport of karate is divided into two areas: *kumite* and *kata*. In contrast with the various types of karate fighters, the *kata* competitor is the one most clearly practising a martial art. Competition karate was originally conceived as a martial art, but increasingly it is more and more a combat sport. As a result the best exponents tend to be big, strong, fast and aggressive, as well as having devastating technique.

*Fig 257   Modern karate competition is extremely well organized and thousands of competitors take part at all levels.*

Why people should want to compete is an interesting question, and there are many theories. The most convincing is one put forward by the psychologist Alfred Adler, a contemporary of Freud and Jung, who invented the term 'inferiority complex' to explain his concept of motivational theory. Basically, we are born as babies who grow into children and then become adults. Adler described how part of this process involves perceiving ourselves as smaller and weaker and vulnerable to other people, and the consequent reaction to this essentially intolerable position, a striving to be better, superior to others. This inferiority complex manifests itself differently in different people, but provides a fairly convincing theory for much of human behaviour, from trying to earn more money, or wanting a bigger car, to wishing to become a karate champion. Despite the negative connotations of the term, it is not necessarily a negative concept, but rather a very positive one, giving both a logical and emotional basis to much of our striving and toiling.

Adler advocated achievement as the balm to feelings of inferiority, which could ultimately lead to self-realization or self-actualisation, as a later psychologist Abraham Maslow put it.

Some karateka see competition as a test of their skill, nerve and conditioning and, need to be reassured as to the effectiveness of what they do in the dojo. Others thrive on the feelings of success that accompany winning competitions and like the congratulations of their peers, friends and families, or even of the media if they reach international level. Some perhaps less successful competitors want to be known as 'tough guys', or at the very least someone not to mess with. Still others are addicted to adrenaline, the surge that goes through them when they face a dangerous opponent in an all or nothing situation. Most competitors are attracted by the notion of the challenge. Some traditional teachers say that training in karate is like forging a sword, but that the sword's true worth can only really be known by testing it in combat. In that sense competition can be seen as a quest for truth, at least for some.

The other aspect of psychology in competition involves knowing your opponents and the style of fighting they favour; whether they prefer to attack or to wait and counter, and the like, so that you can devise appropriate tactics to defeat them.

## Styles of Competition

Free-fighting competition is called *shiai* and is for many people the most exciting part of doing karate. The most widespread and popular form of karate competition is the semi-contact type, where blows are delivered in controlled fashion with no deliberate attempt to hurt or injure, or knock out the opponent. None of the systems under which karate competitions take place are perfect; efforts are continually being made to improve them and anyone interested in competing is well advised to go along and see what awaits them, rather than just turning up and having a go. Proper preparation and conditioning is absolutely essential, as is familiarity with the rules and regulations in order to be able to compete in relative safety. The varying demands of the activities and their disparate rule structures can also make a big difference to how effective you as an individual can be, depending upon what your particular strengths and weaknesses are.

Even in semi-contact, because of the danger of injury from uncontrolled techniques there are repeated calls for body protectors, headguards and the like to make the sport safer. Most competitors wear shinpads, safety mitts, groin protectors and gum-shields as it is, in an effort to minimize the risk of injury. Many full contact fighters say that their sport is actually safer than semi-contact, because they know exactly what to expect and there is no question of having to trust the other person to hold back or of being accidentally knocked out by a bare fist!

Nerves can get the better of even the most accomplished fighters. At the European championships in Genoa in 1988, which was a semi-contact event, a Danish competitor, Frank Bura, in the opening seconds of his first contest, front kicked his luckless opponent in the body and followed up with a lunge punch to the face. The result was two broken ribs and a broken jaw. The Danish fighter got disqualified from the rest of the competition and the other competitor was taken off on a stretcher, unconscious, so both of them ended up losers. The problem of safety and contact in semi-contact is then very real.

The Kyokushinkai style compete in knockdown championships which are open to all styles. The knockdown type of fighting takes place on a mat and allows full power throwing techniques too, although groundwork is not permitted. Punching techniques to the face are not allowed, because the whole event would rapidly degenerate into a bloodbath and serious injuries would be inevitable. The bare fist can do far more damage than the boxer's glove to unprotected flesh and bone. Nevertheless to compete at a knockdown championships requires good conditioning and considerable physical courage. Even the winners know that they are going to suffer a fair amount of physical punishment in the process.

Full contact karate is on a par with amateur boxing as a realistic, athletically demanding form of combat sport. It takes place in a ring, with the competitors wearing gloves and sometimes headguards. Full contact has its equivalent professional ranks, sometimes called kickboxing. Real Muay Thai kickboxing, however, is a lot harder and more brutal, especially in the professional ranks, where serious injuries and deaths are a lot more commonplace than in western professional boxing.

The style of karate a person chooses to do is often dictated by chance. It is a rare individual who is aware of the variety of styles and emphases that exists if he is not already involved in the activity. The vast majority of participants do semi-contact karate and the first thing anyone intending to compete needs to know are the rules, points scoring system and requirements of etiquette. As

*Fig 258   A karate contest is a physical clash that requires  considerable courage and fighting spirit. Any weaknesses, whether of spirit, technique or as in this case, stance, will be found out and punished.*

karate is a Japanese sport, it is also necessary to know some Japanese, at the very least the commands used by the referee.

## ETIQUETTE AND DISCIPLINE

In karate etiquette is very important. It is part of a system of discipline that is absolutely vital to the future of the activity. Bill Wallace once said "Discipline is a state of mind, not just the process of training." If you fight someone else in competition it is your responsibility to treat them and all officials with the respect they deserve. You represent yourself, your teachers, your club and sometimes even your area or country. There is no shame in being beaten or even robbed by a bad decision, but there is no excuse for letting yourself down. When the essential mental control and courtesy is absent, the results can be disastrous. One of the greatest moments of shame in the history of karate happened in 1977 in Long Beach, USA, when the brilliant French champion Dominique Valera lost control after a decision was given against him and attacked the referees. His actions provoked a riot as dozens of spectators and competitors got caught up in the situation and the police had to be called to calm things down. Valera was arrested, imprisoned and subsequently banned from competing for life. Whatever the rights and wrongs of the refereeing decision might have been, they paled into insignificance compared with Valera's gross misconduct.

Referees are only human and can make mistakes like anyone else. Generally, they do their best and try to be unbiased, everyone has bad decisions go against them, but the law of averages means that sometimes they go in your favour too, perhaps when you do not deserve it. The element of chance, of luck cannot be removed from sports, and without it there would be little interest. Fortunes can change dramatically on the day of a competition. That is part of the interest. The Valera incident was unwholesome and reflected

badly on the karate world, giving the general public the impression that many top class karateka were no better than hooligans.

On other occasions the failure to observe proper behaviour has had tragic consequences. Top karateka who should know better have been involved in incidents where people have been wounded and even killed. Karate can make someone into a formidable adversary, but it does not make them invulnerable. A British karate team member was shot dead by police in Spain as a result of an incident in a night club in the 1970s.

An important part of etiquette is the bow. Competitors bow to one another to start a contest and to end it. They normally shake hands at the end of a bout, too. They also bow to the officials refereeing their bouts – usually a referee, arbitrator and judge (sometimes there are four corner judges and a referee who moves around with the competitors). Any disrespect towards your opponent or the officials will result in penalization and/ or disqualification, if considered serious and this extends outside the mat area to the rest of the competition arena. Disrespectful behaviour at a karate competition is totally unacceptable. This applies to your club and team mates, spectators, family and friends, and extends to everyone present at the event. Verbal abuse, barracking, foul language or rude behaviour cannot and will not be tolerated. Remember: 'Karate begins and ends with courtesy'.

## RULES

The rules of karate competition are very complicated, and different associations have their own rule books available for reference and study. Some of the basic rules include guidelines on the fighting area, protective equipment, control, excessive contact, and what determines an effective technique. Most of the rules are concerned with ensuring the personal safety of the competitor and make very good sense. The standard fighting areas as described by the World Union of Karate

*Fig 259   Elwyn Hall, one of the finest footsweep exponents in British karate scoring with a footsweep and punch combination. Note how his opponent defends instinctively by grabbing and entangling the sweeping leg and trying to kick from the floor.*

Organizations (WUKO) is a matted area eight metres square, which includes a two-metre safety area. Competition should always be held on mats for the safety of competitors, to reduce the risk of back injuries, head injuries, concussions and the like, as a result of falling. Hand mitts are compulsory in all WUKO-organized competitions and men have to wear a box. Shin protectors and instep guards are often optional.

An individual contest or bout normally lasts for three minutes, not including stoppage time. Bouts for women and youngsters (under 21) are a minute shorter. Normally, whenever fighting stops (whenever the referee calls *yame*) the clock is stopped and starts again when the referee says *hajime*. As crowd noise is sometimes a problem, the referee normally accompanies his commands with a visual hand signal. It is up to the competitor

to learn to recognize these before entering his first competition. A bell or buzzer will sound thirty seconds before the end of the contest and then again when that time has expired, to signal the end of the bout. The ideal is to score three full points before the three minutes elapses. These points can be straight *ippons* or *waza-aris*, or combinations of both. If the full three points are not achieved, the person with the most points wins. Techniques attempted outside the area or after the final buzzer has sounded will not be scored. A draw is possible in team events, but not in individual contests. If scores are even, the referee consults the judges to decide if a decision can be given on the basis of obvious superiority. If such is not the case an *echo-sen*, a sudden-death two or three minute extension will be called for and the first to score will win. A full point is awarded for a perfect technique, or a very good attempt at an especially difficult or spectacular one that takes the opponent by surprise. Half points are awarded

*Fig 260   For those who like to compete, but have no desire to do free fighting, there are kata competitions.*

for almost perfect techniques to the opponent's head, chest, midsection and back.

Only the lightest contact is allowed to the opponent's face and excessive contact will be penalized by *keikoku*, which is the equivalent of a *waza-ari* to your opponent. If contact was only very slight you may only get a verbal warning, but it is possible to be instantly disqualified, depending upon the referee's interpretation of the situation. Wrestling, judo, pushing and shoving is not allowed in karate, and you may be penalized for trying it. You are not allowed to threaten, talk to, swear at or in any way attempt to intimidate your opponent. On no account argue with the referee's decision, even if you think it is totally wrong. If your coach or teacher thinks the decision was unjust the proper procedure is to put in a written complaint. If both competitors land effective techniques simultaneously, no score is given, and the referee signals this by saying *aiuchi* and putting his fists together.

*Fig 261   World Champion José Egea of Spain, taking care to keep warm and flexible between bouts, here practising his mawashi-geri.*

## POINT SCORING AND PENALTIES

The aim of competition is quite simple: to score a point on your opponent with a controlled, recognized and legally permitted technique, while preventing him from scoring on you. 'Controlled' is the key word here. Many people can do hard, fast techniques, but the really testing element, the real skill, lies in focusing and controlling the technique. A karate contest is not a fight. It is an athletic contest, the aim of which is to defeat your opponent by showing superior skill. Psychological pressures and nerves obviously make this more difficult than it sounds.

Many techniques are not allowed in competition, and certain areas are off-limits, including kicking to the knees or groin, straight finger attacks to the face and throat and many others which are considered too difficult or dangerous to be effectively controlled. Curiously enough, 80 per cent of injuries come from uncontrolled punches to the face. Drawing blood is not accept-able and usually results in disqualification, unless your opponent was considered to have been negligent in some way. At one time, blood meant automatic disqualification, but human nature being what it is this led to people moving their heads into range deliberately, in order to ensure they got hit, the logic being that a gold medal was worth a split lip or a bloody nose – tactics gone mad! As a result competitors were instructed that they must take proper precautions to keep themselves safe from injury when attacking (a bit like the clause in boxing that says you must defend yourself at all times). This concept, called *mubobi*, means that referees have a certain amount of leeway. If they think a competitor has been negligent or deliberately set out to get hit in order to get his opponent disqualified, they can rule accidental contact. A knockout blow to the head usually means definite disqualification for lack of control, but quite heavy contact to the body is allowed. It is a good idea, therefore, for all competitors to have well-conditioned mid-sections.

*Fig 262 Perfect timing, a daring jump and fast hands allow this surprise punch to the face to get past the defender's block and score.*

Gum shields, too, are a good idea, though not compulsory.

Originally, karate competitions were of the *shobu ippon* type and some championships are still run this way. This means that the first competitor to score with a perfect technique, the single lethal blow so often talked about in karate circles, would win the match. The thinking behind it is that the technique, were it not controlled, would result in serious injury or death. A not-quite-perfect technique would fail to get the decisive *ippon* score that ends the bout, but might earn a *waza-ari*, or half point, two half points equalling *ippon*. The sudden death nature of *shobu ippon* can make matches very boring to watch, however, as a single mistake can mean it is all over, and fighters tend not to be very adventurous as a result.

In an effort to make the sport more spectator oriented, WUKO introduced *shobu sanbon*, or three-point contest. This was originally won on a best of three points basis and later developed into what it is today, a genuine three-point contest, where a competitor must score three full points to win. The effect of this was to open up the range of techniques used, and to encourage a positive attacking style that makes competitions much more varied and interesting to watch. In the early days coaches were allowed to give advice to their players at matside and even argue with refereeing panels as bouts were going on. This lead to no end of problems, so the coach is no longer allowed matside.

*Jogai* means exit, or stepping out of the competition area, which happens quite often if a player gets ahead and goes on the defensive, running backwards to escape an opponent's attacks in an effort to waste time. The first time you step out you get a verbal warning, the second time you concede a half point, the third time a full point. If you do it a fourth time, you lose the match. This can be an important aspect of tactics, with matches being won and lost as a result.

## WEIGHT CATEGORIES

Karate competitions take place in the following weight categories:

**Men**

Super-lightweight – under 60kg
Lightweight – under 65kg
Light-middleweight – under 70kg
Middleweight – under 75kg
Light heavyweight – under 80kg
Heavyweight – over 80kg
Open weight – any weight

**Women**

Lightweight – under 43kg
Middleweight – under 53kg
Heavyweight – over 60kg

**Young men (under 21)**

Super-lightweight – under 60kg
Lightweight – under 65kg
Middleweight – under 70kg
Light heavyweight – under 75kg
Heavyweight – over 75kg

# FITNESS TRAINING FOR COMPETITION

Fitness, or cardiovascular training, is of prime importance to karateka, but fortunately there are a variety of interesting and enjoyable ways to get a good cardiovascular effect. Weight training has already been considered. Running, cycling, skipping, swimming and taking part in other sports are probably the most enjoyable and sociable ways to achieve this, though the main difficulty is finding somewhere to play these other sports at an enjoyable but not too serious level. Football and basketball are good sports for general fitness, but most social teams expect members to turn up for training a couple of times a week, which you may not have time to do if you are committed to doing karate three nights a week. A good alternative to team sports which demand a high commitment are sports like badminton and squash, which are offered at most sports centres. The big advantage of individual sports like running, cycling and swimming is that you can do these on your own if no one else feels like joining you.

If you are not interested in learning about exercise physiology and do not want to do boring circuits, but just want to play sports to keep fit, that is fine. However, when considering the question of fitness you have to ask the question 'fit for what?' A marathon runner has tremendous endurance and can run extremely long distances at considerable speeds. While this means he has a superb cardiovascular base, it does not mean he is ready to take part in a full contact bout. Likewise, a national class sprinter can run very fast over short distances but he too is in no sense automatically fit for a full contact bout.

## Running

In semi-contact karate the kind of fitness needed is largely aerobic with bursts of anaerobic activity. The greater the stress a karateka is under in a contest the more likely he is to be required to work anaerobically. Full contact fighters will tend to do a lot more anaerobic work when in clinches, where the opponent may hold and hang on them to make breathing difficult. In both cases it is necessary to develop a good level of basic muscular endurance without sacrificing speed. Endurance is the capacity to keep going when doing physical exercise or work. The kind of work or exercise done for endurance training is often referred to as low intensity or steady state work, because it is carried out at a sustainable level, depending for energy supply on the body's aerobic system.

High intensity work, such as 100m and 400m sprints, is almost purely anaerobic. Anaerobic work leaves the athlete breathless, suffering from large build-ups of lactic acid in the muscles, and unable to continue without a recovery period of some form. Sprinting is particularly beneficial to karateka and can be made more interesting by training in groups of four or five. Try going for a track session and doing four to six 400m sprints, with five minutes rest between each one, or on the next occasion, doing eight to twelve 100m dashes. Although the actual time spent exercising is, in the first case, no more than six or seven minutes, and in the second, probably less than two, the intensity of the exercise is shattering and the effects on your speed and anaerobic fitness training, say twice a week over a twelve week period, can be dramatic.

How is general endurance improved? Quite simply, by getting your heart rate up to 70 or 80 per cent of your maximum and sustaining it in that range for at least twelve minutes in the case of the unfit, and up to an hour and a half in well-trained athletes. Training for longer than one and a half hours is only required in pure high endurance sports, like marathon running and triathlon. Training has to be tailored to individual needs, of course. Excessive endurance training will burn muscle in the upper body, probably leading to a loss of power and speed, and may well cause a deterioration in flexibility. It can also have an adverse effect on joints, so be warned.

A very unfit person or complete beginner would need to do about eight weeks of gentle preparation training at about 60 to 70 per cent of maximum pulse rate for relatively short periods. The average black belt can benefit from going for a twenty to forty minute run, trying to sustain a six-minute-mile pace, either on the track or cross country. Road running is convenient for many people, but running on hard surfaces can have a jarring effect on the joints. Make sure you run in a well-padded pair of shoes and if you notice any pain in knees, ankles or hips switch to some other form of training.

As well as going for steady pace runs, variable pace running can be beneficial. The Swedish word 'Fartlek' is often used to describe this kind of training, which was largely pioneered by Scandinavian athletes. Basically, it can involve jogging for thirty seconds then striding for thirty seconds. On the track, try slow jogging the bends and sprinting the straights, or vice-versa. Combat sports athletes generally like this kind of training because in many ways it can reflect the rhythm and pace changes often encountered in their training sessions and contests. In a national championships you might have to compete against someone vastly inferior in the first round, and the world champion in the next; you always need to be able to raise your game!

## Pulse Rate and Fitness

Pulse rate and speed of recovery from exertion can be used as a guide to ascertain levels of fitness and before embarking on a fitness improvement programme it is necessary to know two things: your resting pulse rate and your theoretical maximum pulse rate. The latter is determined by simply subtracting your age from the figure 220. Thus, a twenty year old has a maximum of 200, a thirty year old 190 a forty year old 180 and so on. The formula to get the range within which your heart should be working is then quite simple, you just have to multiply the maximum by 70 and

then by 80 per cent. Thus, a twenty year old would train at between 140 and 160 beats per minute; a thirty year old between 133 and 152 beats per minute, and a forty year old between 126 and 144 beats per minute. To determine your resting pulse rate you take your pulse first thing in the morning before you get out of bed. Take your pulse by pressing lightly with your index and middle fingers against the vein in the wrist just below the base of the thumb on the thumb side of your forearm. Count the beats, small, regular pulsations made by the blood pumping through a valve in the vein, for a full minute, timing yourself against a clock.

The national average is 72 for a man and 84 for a woman. In trained individuals, generally, the lower the pulse rate, the higher the index of aerobic fitness. Professional athletes often have resting pulse rate in the low thirties, and many fitness tests have been devised which calculate fitness on the basis of how soon the heart rate returns to normal after exercise. Many factors can affect pulse rate, such as: exercise, nervousness, tension, fear, desire and even having a drink or eating a meal can all trigger chemical and hormonal reactions which affect your pulse.

Once you are familiar with the technique of taking your pulse you can quickly monitor how hard your heart is working by taking a count over fifteen seconds, again using a watch, and multiply the result by four. This is easy to do during rest periods in circuits or when exercising on an ergometer or stationary bicycle, but can cause accidents on running machines and treadmills, so be careful.

Gymnasium based and dojo based cardiovascular circuits are illustrated in figures 244 and 245 on page 130.

Additional training is hard work and sometimes it can be very difficult to fit in with other commitments, but anyone hoping to reach the top in competitive karate has to do it.

# 7  Karate Weapons

*'Learning is the gate, not the house. When you see the gate don't
think it is the house. You have to go through the gate to get to the
house which is behind it.'*

Miyamoto Musashi

It may seem anomalous to some that the martial art of karate-do, which is translated as 'empty hand way' does in fact involve training, or at least. dabbling, with weapons in many styles. The weapons of traditional karate are Okinawan weapons: the *bo*, *tonfa*, *nunchaku*, *kama* and *sai*. The origins of these weapons and the reasons for their inclusion in karate training are historical and practical. The *nunchaku*, *kama* and *tonfa* were all originally farming implements and as the ownership of real weapons, such as swords, daggers, spears and bows and arrows was prohibited on Okinawa, first by the Okinawan rulers themselves and later by the Japanese, their development as weapons was determined more by circumstance than by any real suitability for the task.

Okinawan *Te* evolved as a system of physical training and preparation for self defence in a society where bearing weapons was forbidden. Although there are many colourful tales of how the Okinawans developed their system of fighting to include secret, unsuspected weapons like the *sai*, *nunchaku* and *tonfa*, to resist and defend themselves against their Japanese oppressors, the more likely truth is that they evolved as weapons for use against other Okinawans. In an agrarian society made up of numerous small villages, people tend to be somewhat clannish, and this is reflected in the comments made by many Okinawan karateka today. Many of the stories about the history of karate on Okinawa revolve around challenges, and wild youngsters attacking older teachers with established reputations in order to prove themselves. An expert could of course defend himself against a single unarmed and undisciplined at-

tacker, even against two or three, but if they had sticks or chains or other types of weapon, it would be advisable for the expert to arm himself too. The obvious solution was to arm oneself with what came to hand – namely, the farming implements used every day in ordinary life. Some Okinawan fishermen even perform *kata* using a rowing boat oar! This improvisation is typically Okinawan, and common in Japanese *budo* too.

While many experts are capable of remarkable displays with such weapons, it has to be realized that they are not really a match for a Japanese longsword in the hands of a trained warrior, armoured or not. Many martial arts clubs succumb to the temptation to put on demonstrations of *sai* against sword or *bo* against sword to impress the public, but they are generally misleading. Any Okinawan fighting with a samurai would have been executed anyway; even Japanese policemen were not allowed to bear weapons. If required to arrest a samurai only the *jitte*, an iron truncheon useful for defending oneself against sword and knife attacks, could be used. The *sai*, which is a weapon of unknown origin that was also used on Okinawa by the police, is capable of being used for defence against an attack with a sword; so is a pick-axe handle, but it is a very uneven contest, heavily favouring the man with the sword.

It is important to keep a sense of perspective about weapons training. All the Okinawan weapons are potentially dangerous and should only be trained with in *kata* and prearranged pair form exercises. Free-fighting with them is extremely dangerous and cannot be recommended because the slightest miscalculation, just a touch, can seriously injure or kill your partner. A sport form of *nunchaku* competition has developed in which the contestants wear protection and strike each other with rubber *nunchaku*, along the lines of semi-contact karate. Really all that is tested is speed and reflexes (which is also a criticism some full contact fighters have levelled against semi-contact karate). Many techniques, such as locking and choking, which have unquestionable value in real combat, simply cannot be applied in the sports format.

When Gichin Funakoshi brought karate to Japan and changed the meaning of its name from 'Chinese hand' to 'empty hand' it was decided that specific weapons training of the kind carried out in dojo on Okinawa would not be included in the new Japanese form of karate. Part of the reason for this was that Japanese *budo* and *bujutsu* already contained a wide variety of weapons training developed by warriors using weapons of war. The average middle class Japanese of Funakoshi's time might have been forgiven for asking himself, 'Why learn to use an Okinawan farmer's sickle to fight with, when you work in a city, not on a farm? If you want to learn to fight with weapons, why not do kendo or kenjutsu and learn how to use a *katana*?' At the end of the day, Japanese society was very class conscious and the weapons practised on Okinawa were peasants' weapons, with no real place in modern Japanese life. Anyway, specific weapons training was left out of the general karate training. Weapons were introduced into the dojo occasionally to demonstrate unarmed combat against armed adversaries and develop disarming and self defence techniques.

Some more eclectic styles of karate include other more strictly Japanese weapons such as the *katana, wakizashi, tanto, aikuchi, tambo, jo, kusarigama, manrikigusari, nunte, naginata, yari, tessen, jitte,* and *yawara,* some of which are illegal even to own. Ninjitsu exponents, too, make a more detailed study of the above weapons. Many karateka train to meet the threat of armed attack using empty hand and foot techniques, simply because in nor-

mal modern day life, people do not walk around carrying weapons and are in fact prevented from doing so by the law. In the USA in particular, the principal concern is to develop effective defences against knife and gun attacks. Some specific techniques are considered in chapter eight, but common factors in all situations where dealing with armed aggression are awareness, taking the initiative away from the attacker, speed and decisiveness.

More and more people are taking up an interest in learning how to use and train with what are really archaic weapons. Their motivation for doing so is varied and at times difficult to explain, but perhaps the real reason for their fascination is that practising with them teaches us more about the minds and attitudes of the people who developed their use in the first place, the old masters who, at times, really did have to use them, in life or death situations. It was generally believed on Okinawa that no karateka who did not train with weapons could be considered expert: to know how to defend yourself against attack with a weapon you must know the weapon. In the hands of experts, these weapons are all extensions of the body and spirit.

## TRADITIONAL OKINAWAN KOBOJUTSU

Traditional Okinawan weapons, like all weapons, are dangerous, especially if used or handled inexpertly. Anyone wishing to learn to use them should seek out qualified instruction and learn to handle them safely. The safe use of all of these weapons presupposes basic competence in the performance of the techniques of Okinawan *Te.*

### The *Bo* (Six Foot Staff)

The *Bo* is a 1.8m (6ft) long hardwood staff, about 2.5cm (1in) in diameter and tapering slightly towards the ends. Staves have often been carried by wayfarers to assist them in making long jour-

*Fig 263    Exponent of Okinawan kobujutsu practising bo kata.*

neys, crossing rough terrain, and to defend themselves against wild animals and bandits. The Okinawan *bo*, however, was originally used for carrying heavy loads, which could be equally distributed on either end of the *bo* and carried more easily either over the shoulder, with the loads in front and behind the body or across the shoulders, to either side of the body. On rough, muddy tracks made slippery by monsoon rains, this was one of the best ways to transport goods to market before the advent of modern transportation, since primitive carts and wheelbarrows would slip and slide in the mud.

Like any quarterstaff, the advantage that the *bo* affords its user is that of reach. It can be used to make jabbing, spear-like attacks with either end or clubbing movements using the length of the weapon. It also lends itself well to blocking attacks made with sticks, clubs and knives, and skilled exponents can trip and sweep their adversaries with a variety of effective techniques. Training with the *bo* is felt to be especially useful in developing movement skills and co-ordination.

The practical usefulness of the *bo* in modern times is virtually null. By walking down the street with a six foot staff, you are unlikely to be attacked, but will probably be arrested instead. However, training done using the *bo* teaches principles of distance and timing, which can be applied, should the need arise, with any long object or stick in a situation where instant arming becomes necessary.

Because of the position it occupies as a traditional cultural artefact, folk dances employing the *bo* are popular on Okinawa although they are different to the martial art forms.

## Nunchaku (Rice Flails)

The *nunchaku* was originally used for pounding and threshing grain or rice, and consisted of a pair of hardwood sticks joined at the tops by a horse hair rope. Because it was very easy to cut the rope with a sword or sharp knife, it was replaced by chain and modern *nunchaku* usually have a

*Fig 264  Training with nunchaku.*

makes it almost impossible for an adversary to come close without being struck. It can also be whirled around above the head and brought crashing down with great force when an attacker tries to come in. The late Bruce Lee, film star and Chinese martial artist, was probably single-handedly responsible for the popularization of the *nunchaku* on a massive scale, as a result of his spectacular and exciting use of them in films like *Enter the Dragon*. It can also be used to block weapons attacks and to catch extended limbs, wrists or ankles in painful, scissoring techniques.

The *nunchaku* is relatively small and easy to conceal, but takes a lot of practice to be able to handle effectively and safely for the user. There have been cases of untrained users buying *nunchaku* and attempting to imitate things they have seen on television or in the cinema, seriously injuring and even killing themselves. A fast swinging, hardwood *nunchaku* striking an unprotected head can easily fracture the skull, and if it strikes a vital point like the temple, it can kill.

chain and swivel attachment or a nylon cord. Training *nunchaku* usually have rounded handles, which makes them easier to grip initially, but combat *nunchaku* are hard edged and octagonal in design, which means that the striking force is more concentrated. Wrist locks and strangles are much more painful when applied with this type of weapon. There are also three- and four-piece *nunchaku*, although their use and practice is a lot less widespread.

The *nunchaku* is a versatile weapon and can be used for blocking, striking, trapping and strangling. It is generally held with one hand high, at about jaw level, the stick resting on the same shoulder as the hand holding it, the chain or cord going under the armpit, and the other stick gripped at the hip with the lower arm covering the abdomen. It can be swung to generate centripetal force and can be used as an extension of the arms to make whip-like striking attacks to the shins, knees, ribs and head of adversaries. Swinging the *nunchaku* in a figure-of-eight pattern,

*Fig 265  The tonfa, a most versatile weapon.*

## *Tonfa* (Wooden Handles)

Called *tuifa* on Okinawa the *tonfa* were originally used for grinding rice and soya, but were among the farm implements most easily adapted to karate. Measuring about 50cm (20in) in length they consist of two oak sticks with handles fitted three-quarters of the way along. The weapons are held by the handles and align with the underside of the forearm. One end aligns with the elbow and the other extends a few inches beyond the fist holding the handle.

The *tonfa* can be used as extensions of the arm and hand to block and strike with. To increase their range they can be reversed, spinning them around the wooden handle. The *tonfa* can be practised alone without any real risk of injuring yourself. Trying to practise with a partner is very dangerous though, and should only be done as preset, pair form work under competent instruction. Many police forces use a single *tonfa* in place of the traditional baton or truncheon, but it is normally lighter than the traditional hardwood weapon, often being made of rubber and plastic compounds, or wood coated with such compounds to reduce its effectiveness. The balance between an effective weapon and one that does not do too much damage is very fine. The *tonfa* is, however, a weapon requiring an effective base in karate training, without which its effectiveness is considerably reduced anyway.

## The *Sai*

The *sai* is a strange weapon. Its origin is unknown, although occasional preposterous stories about it being used to plant rice (misconstrued by people who have never seen how rice is planted, naturally) do crop up in some dojos. *Sai*-like weapons exist in India, China and throughout south-east Asia. It is basically a form of defensive dagger. Some of these weapons have sharpened blades and points, others are cylindrical and blunted. The blunted kind are those used in karate practice. The *sai* has a central prong and a hilt with two shorter, curving prongs designed to catch bladed weapons or sticks. It is normally held by the handle but can be manipulated to perform a variety of blocks and strikes. It can be used to jab with, like a pointed weapon, to punch with and to block with. *Sai* are quite heavy, but experts can manipulate them at great speed and they greatly augment the striking force of a karate blow. Again, they are said to have been used on Okinawa by the police and officials to hold back crowds and arrest people, and were felt to be effective against *bo*, *tonfa*, *kama* and *nunchaku*. It is also claimed that they can be used to defend against sword attacks, but having witnessed the speed and power of both weapons in the hands of experts, the author's opinion is that the *bushi*, or samurai, wielding the sword would have to have been drunk for the policeman with the *sai* to have been able to arrest him – which might well have been the case on more than one occasion!

*Fig 266  Expert performing kata with sai.*

151

Many practitioners feel doing *kata* with *sai* has the same effect as using wrist weights, and helps improve musculature and power as well as concentration.

## Kama (Sickle)

The *kama*, or short sickle, is a vicious-looking implement originally used for farming purposes, but which can be swung like a curved axe to slash or stab an adversary. Often two *kama* are used simultaneously, one in each hand, with one held low, and the other held high. They can be used defensively to catch incoming strikes, but also make lethal offensive weapons. The real agricultural *kama*, while razor sharp, was relatively flimsy and would not have been robust enough to withstand a determined attack with *bo*, *nunchaku* or *tonfa*. However, it has been conjectured that fighting *kama*, of a much stronger, heavier variety were probably secretly manufactured and kept in easily accessible places. Even if employed in daily use, they would have been indistinguishable from the normal farming tool, especially to a bureaucratic official with little knowledge of farmers' tools. In training, real metal *kama* are not generally used for safety reasons: one mistake could result in a partner's fingers being chopped off. Some schools practise pair form *kata* with *kama* that have no points or sharpened edges, but the majority prefer to train with wooden, dummy *kama*.

The point where blade and handle intersect is often used for trapping weapons, and in training, the *bo* is generally used against the *kama*. Some feudal kata have survived to the present day, including *Shozan*, *Kanigawa sho* and *Kanigawa-dai*. The practice of pair form *kata* is only for the most experienced exponents, and requires great control and precision. Free-fighting is absolutely out of the question as serious injury or death would be the likely result.

## OTHER 'KARATE WEAPONS'

Some other weapons which are not traditional Okinawan weapons, but which were used for centuries by various Japanese *bujutsu ryu*, are sometimes studied in karate dojo, though they are not, strictly speaking, karate weapons. The weapons techniques of the Japanese *ryu* such as the *katori-ryu* and the *kashima-ryu* employ a much more complicated use of strategy than is observable in the Okinawan styles. Many of the techniques of these schools were kept secret, and outsiders were not allowed to view training sessions. Some of these weapons are terrible in their savage effectiveness, one of the most prominent being the *kusarigama* (chain and sickle).

*Fig 267 The most dangerous of the Okinawan karate weapons for the unskilled trainee: the kama or sickle.*

## *Kusarigama* (Chain and Sickle)

One *kama* or sickle was sometimes used by joining it to a chain in certain martial arts schools, and was called the *kusarigama*, or chain and sickle (*kusari*, meaning 'chain', and *kama*, meaning 'sickle'). This is a particularly deadly combination as the chain, which sometimes had a metal ball on the other end, could be anything from 1 to 2m ( 3 – 7ft) long and could be used to lash out at an adversary at a distance, swinging the metal ball around like a mace and throwing it at him. The weapon would not be lost even if it missed, because it remained attached to the chain, so could be easily recovered. The chain could also be used to entangle an adversary, or to strangle him, and he could then be finished off on the ground with the sickle.

## Secret techniques

According to tradition members of different schools often challenged one another to life or death duels, so keeping one's techniques a secret was a matter of deadly seriousness. Sometimes teachers even taught deliberate mistakes to their students, in case they should be spies or defect at some future date, and give away what they had learned and sworn to keep secret. This would also mean that if the teacher were challenged by someone thinking he had discovered the flaw in his style, he would be prepared for their effort to exploit the perceived weakness and would have suitable tactics ready to deal with his adversary. The capacity to mystify, to distort and disguise strengths and weaknesses, is a very Japanese characteristic and part of their strategy in warfare and business. It should not be underestimated.

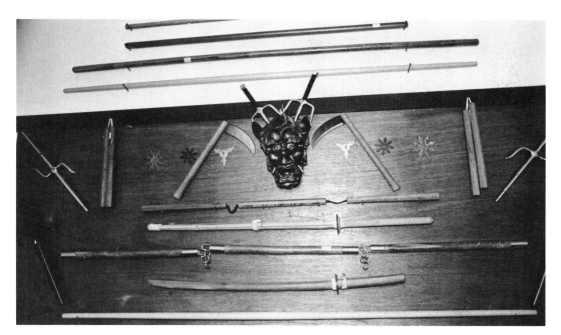

*Fig 268    A selection of typical karate weapons that might be found in any dojo.*

*Fig 269   Higaonna sensei 8th dan, explaining the correct points of wrist and forearm contact for effective blocking to black belt students.*

*Figs 270–271   Throws and joint-locking techniques are taught in traditional karate for their self-defence value.*
*Here Goju-Ryu's Higaonna Sensei demonstrates a variety of techniques to other karateka on a Goju-Ryu training course.*

# Glossary

| | |
|---|---|
| **Age-zuki** | Rising punch |
| **Age-uke** | Rising block |
| **Aka** | Red |
| **Ashi-barai** | Foot-sweep |
| **Ashibo-kake-ashi** | Hooking leg block |
| **Ashi-gake** | Foot hook |
| **Ashi-waza** | Foot sweeps |
| **Ate-waza** | Smashing technique |
| **Awase-zuki** | U-punch |
| **Choku-zuki** | Straight punch |
| **Chudan** | Chest area |
| **Ch'uan fa** | Chinese hand |
| **Dan-zuki** | Consecutive punching |
| **Dojo** | Training hall |
| **Empi** | Elbow |
| **Empi-uchi** | Elbow strike |
| **Fudo-dachi** | Rooted stance |
| **Fumikiri** | Cutting kick |
| **Fumikomi** | Stamping, stepping in |
| **Fumi-waza** | Stamping techniques |
| **Gedan** | Lower body |
| **Gedan-barai** | Downward block |
| **Gedan-kekomi** | Thrust kick to groin |
| **Gedan-zuki** | Punch to groin |
| **Geta** | Clogs |
| **Gyaku-mawashi-geri** | Reverse roundhouse kick |
| **Gyaku-zuki** | Reverse punch |
| **Hachiji-dachi** | Open legged stance |
| **Haishu** | Back of the hand |
| **Haishu-uchi** | Back of the hand strike |
| **Haisoku** | Instep |
| **Haito** | Ridge-hand |
| **Haito-uchi** | Ridge-hand strike |
| **Hajime** | Begin |
| **Hangetsu-dachi** | Hourglass stance |
| **Hanmi** | Half front facing |
| **Hansoku** | Foul |
| **Hansoku chui** | One point penalty |
| **Hantei** | Decision |
| **Hasami-zuki** | Scissors punch |
| **Heiko-dachi** | Parallel stance |
| **Heisoku-dachi** | Informal attention stance |
| **Hidari** | Left |
| **Hidari-shizentai** | Left natural posture |
| **Hiji** | Elbow |
| **Hiji-ate** | Elbow-smash |
| **Hiji-uchi** | Elbow strike |
| **Hiraken** | Fore knuckle fist |
| **Hizagashira** | Kneecap |
| **Ippon** | Full point |
| **Ippon-ken** | One-knuckle fist |
| **Jiyu-kumite** | Freestyle sparring |
| **Jodan** | Face area |
| **Jodan-age-uke** | Upper block vs. head attack |
| **Jodan-choku-zuki** | Straight punch to the head |
| **Jodan-kekomi** | Thrust kick to face |
| **Jogai** | Outside area |
| **Jo-sokutei** | Raised sole of foot. |
| **Juji-uke** | X-block |
| **Kagi-zuki** | Hook punch |
| **Kaisho** | Open hand |
| **Kakato** | Heel |
| **Kake-shuto-uke** | Hooking knife hand block |
| **Kake-uke** | Hooking block |
| **Kakiwake-uke** | Wedge block |
| **Kakuto** | Bent wrist |
| **Karate** | Empty hand |
| **Karate-do** | Way of the empty hand |
| **Kata** | Forms |

| | | | |
|---|---|---|---|
| **Keage** | Snap kick | **Neko-ashi-dachi** | Cat stance |
| **Keikoku** | Half point penalty | **Nidan-geri** | Double-footed jump kick |
| **Keito-uke** | Chicken head bent wrist block | **Nihon-nukite** | Two-fingered spear hand |
| **Kekomi** | Thrust kick | **Nukite** | Spear hand |
| **Kendo** | Way of the sword | **Oi-zuki** | Lunge punch, stepping punch |
| **Kentsui** | Hammer-fist | **Osae-uke** | Pressing block |
| **Keri** | Kick | **Otoshi-empi-uchi** | Downward elbow strike |
| **Keri-waza** | Kicking techniques | **Otoshi-uke** | Dropping block |
| **Kesa-geri** | Diagonal kick | **Otoshi-hiji-ate** | Downward elbow strike |
| **Kiba-dachi** | Straddle or horse stance | **Reinoji-dachi** | L-stance |
| **Kihon kumite** | Prearranged sparring | **Renzoku-geri** | Combination kicking |
| **Kiken** | Withdrawal | **Renzuki** | Alternate punching |
| **Kizami-zuki** | Jab | **Sanchin-dachi** | Hourglass stance |
| **Kokutsu-dachi** | Back stance | **Sanren-zuki** | Triple consecutive punches |
| **Ko-shi** | Ball of the foot | **Seiken-choku-zuki** | Straight forefist punch |
| **Kumade** | Bear hand | | |
| **Kumite** | Sparring | **Seiryotu** | Ox-jaw |
| **Ma-ai** | Distance | **Shiho-wari** | Breaking boards on four sides |
| **Mae-empi-uchi** | Forward elbow strike | **Shikkaku** | Disqualification |
| **Mae-geri** | Front kick | **Shiko-dachi** | Square stance |
| **Mae-geri-keage** | Front snap kick | **Shiro** | White |
| **Mae-geri-kekomi** | Forward thrust kick | **Shittsui** | Knee-hammer |
| **Mae-hij-ate** | Forward elbow strike | **Shizen-tai** | Natural posture |
| **Mae-tobi-geri** | Jumping front kick | **Shobu** | Extension (referring to contest time) |
| **Makiwara** | Punching board or post | | |
| **Mawashi-geri** | Roundhouse kick | **Shuto** | Knife hand |
| **Mawashi-zuki** | Roundhouse punch | **Shuto-uchi** | Knife hand strike |
| **Migi** | Right | **Shuto-uke** | Knife hand block |
| **Mikazki-geri** | Crescent kick | **Sochin-dachi** | Diagonal horse stance |
| **Morote-sukui-uke** | Two-handed scooping block | **Sokutei-mawashi-uke** | Roundhouse block with sole of foot |
| **Morote-tsukami-uke** | Two-handed grasping block | **Sokutei-osae-uke** | Pressing block with sole of foot |
| **Morote-uke** | Two-handed block | | |
| **Morote-zuki** | Double fisted punch | **Sokuto** | Edge of foot |
| **Moto no ichi** | Return to starting line | **Sokuto-keage** | Snap-kick with edge of foot |
| **Musabi-dachi** | Informal attention stance | **Sokuto-osae-uke** | Pressing block with edge of foot |
| **Mubobi** | Failure to ensure one's own safety | | |
| | | **Soto-uke** | Outer block |
| **Nagashi-uke** | Sweeping block | **Suki** | Opening |
| **Nagashi-zuki** | Flowing punch | **Sukui-uke** | Scooping block |
| **Nadaka-ippon-ken** | Middle finger extended knuckle fist | | |

| | |
|---|---|
| **Tameshiwari** | Breaking tests |
| **Tanden** | Navel |
| **Tate-empi-uchi** | Upward elbow strike |
| **Tate-hiji-ate** | Upward elbow strike |
| **Tate-shuto-uke** | Vertical knife hand block |
| **Tate-zuki** | Vertical fist |
| **Teji-dachi** | T-stance |
| **Teisho** | Palm heel |
| **Teisho-uchi** | Palm heel strike |
| **Teisho-uke** | Palm heel block |
| **Tobi-keri** | Jumping kick |
| **Tobi-yoko-geri** | Jumping side kick |
| **Tsukami-uke** | Grasping block |
| **Tsuki** | Punching |
| **Tsuki-waza** | Punching techniques |
| **Tsumasaki** | Tips of toes |
| **Tsuzukete hajime** | Restart contest |
| **Uchi** | Striking |
| **Uchi-uke** | Inner block |
| **Uchi-waza** | Striking techniques |
| **Ude** | Forearm |
| **Ude-uke** | Forearm block |
| **Uke** | Blocking |
| **Uraken** | Backfist |
| **Uraken-uchi** | Backfist strike |
| **Ura-zuki** | Close punch |
| **Ushiro-geri** | Back or rear kick |
| **Ushiro-empi-uchi** | Rear elbow strike |
| **Ushiro-hiji-ate** | Rear elbow smash |
| **Wan** | Arm |
| **Washide** | Eagle head hand |
| **Waza-ari** | Half point |
| **Yama-zuki** | U-punch |
| **Yamei** | Stop |
| **Yoko** | Side |
| **Yoko-empi-uchi** | Side elbow strike |
| **Yoko-geri** | Side kick |
| **Yoko-geri-keage** | Side snap kick |
| **Yoko-geri-kekomi** | Side thrust kick |
| **Yoko-hiji-ate** | Side elbow smash |
| **Yoko-tobi-geri** | Jumping side kick |
| **Zenkutsu-dachi** | Front or forward stance |
| **Zori** | Straw dojo slippers |

# Index